T0334757

THE WORD BECAME CULTURE

DISRUPTIVE CARTOGRAPHERS:
DOING THEOLOGY LATINAMENTE

Series editors: Carmen M. Nanko-Fernández,
Miguel H. Díaz, Gary Riebe-Estrella

This multivolume series re-maps theology and pushes out in new directions from varying coordinates across a spectrum of latinidad as lived in the USA. Authors reconfigure and disrupt key areas like revelation, pneumatology, eschatology, and Mariology. Other volumes complicate and advance even further key themes of significance in Latin@ theologies, including the option for culture, religious diversity, and the integral relationship between theologizing and praxis.

Disruptive Cartographers: Doing Theology Latinamente

THE WORD BECAME CULTURE

MIGUEL H. DÍAZ

Fordham University Press
New York   2024

Fordham University Press has no responsibility for the persistence or accuracy of URLs
for external or third-party Internet websites referred to in this publication and does not
guarantee that any content on such websites is, or will remain, accurate or appropriate.

Fordham University Press also publishes its books in a variety of electronic formats.
Some content that appears in print may not be available in electronic books.

Visit us online at www.fordhampress.com.

Library of Congress Cataloging-in-Publication Data
available online at https://catalog.loc.gov.

Printed in the United States of America
26 25 24 5 4 3 2 1
First Fordham University Press edition, 2024

CONTENTS

v

Preface to the Series

Disruptive Cartographers

Maps are functional and aesthetic. They establish and make visible place, space, time, and distance in terms of scale and relationships that are inevitably influenced by the cartographer's own coordinates. Mapping as a process is not as objective as it might seem, and the maps produced are not beyond bias. Maps are tools of power employed by empires to mark and represent their domains, territorially, economically, politically, culturally, religiously. Mapping also orients resistance by contesting borders, shifting perspective, challenging omissions, retrieving what was rendered invisible or insignificant, disrupting the illusion that certain maps or particular ways of mapping are necessarily normative.

Disruptive Cartographers is a multivolume series mapping theology from varying coordinates across a spectrum of latinidad as lived in the USA. Points of departure for Latin@ theologies are embedded in the complexities of la vida cotidiana, daily lived experience, which call forth a rich variety of responses from theologians who self-identify, in roots and commitments, as belonging to and emerging from the diversity found under such umbrella terms as Hispanic, Latino/a, Latinx, Latin@, Latin@. Explorations of lo cotidiano require a variety of lenses that must take into account intricate historical constructions that cannot easily shake off legacies of racism, sexism, heterosexism, classism, ableism, and colonialism. These legacies and their contemporary manifestations continue to influence sociopolitical contexts, theological formulations, and power and privilege differentials in church, academy, and society. The authors in this series have been left free to choose their own lenses and to probe those historical trajectories which most reflect their experience of the subject at hand.

In this series in constructive theology some volumes seek to reconfigure such key areas as revelation, pneumatology, and eschatology, and others pursue themes significant in theologizing latinamente, including the option for culture, religious pluralism, and the relationship between theory and praxis. Each volume retrieves sources from within the historical stream of Latin@ theologies using contemporary experience as a guide. This series is not an introduction to Latino/a theology; it is not a comprehensive survey of contemporary Latinx theology; it is not an attempt to assert a monolithic or foundational Latin@ theology. Each volume offers a distinctive perspective on a topic familiar to systematic theologians. Accomplished latinamente, each reveals the complexity, diversity, and theological creativity that continues to emerge from within the community of Latino, Latina, Latinx theologians and scholars.

This distinctiveness is evident across the series volumes in a variety of ways. Within Latin@ theologies, socially locating one's perspective is an ethical obligation, an admission that our complicated identities and situated places from which we theologize form, inform, and reform our scholarship. Our fluid identities are expressed through a multiplicity of terms by which we name ourselves (Latino/a, Latinao, Latinoa, Latin@, Latin@, Latinx, Hispanic, Hispana, Hispano, Chican@, Tejana, Boricua, Cuban American are but a few). This self-naming is not a matter of semantics or political correctness but a claim that identity is a matter of theological anthropology. In this series there is no one imposed term, and each author provides their own rationale for their preferences. In addition, Latin@ theologies operate at the intersection of languages, and this hybridity may be reflected in the deployment of English, Spanish, and variations of Spanglish within texts. For Latinos/as Spanish is not a foreign language, and authors may choose not to italicize it in their respective volumes. Our preference for footnotes over endnotes reflects an understanding that they engage in a conversation literally on the same page as the body text. In this (at times) multilingual *conjunto* each maintains its integrity, and it is easier for readers to move from one to the other smoothly.

While each volume offers a distinctive and not a comprehensive perspective, authors situate themselves within the larger enterprise of doing theology latinamente and demonstrate that commitment by underscoring the relevance of lived experience as locus theologicus and by retrieving resources that draw from the depth and breadth of latinidad. Readers can begin their reading with any of the volumes in this series. Their commonality is to be found in the methods authors use to theologize; their diversity is in the historical sources and daily experience they privilege.

Ultimately, this series acknowledges that theological mapping matters for our communities of accountability too long left off or consigned to the margins of too many maps. At the same time, by allowing for creative and sustained development of constructive theological threads, familiar yet new, this series seeks to emulate the advice of Pope Francis to theologians: "Do not lose the ability for wonder; to practice theology in wonder."[1]

Carmen M. Nanko-Fernández,
Gary Riebe-Estrella, Miguel H. Díaz
Series Editors

---

[1] Pope Francis, "Audience with Members of the Italian Theological Association," December 29, 2017, http://press.vatican.va/content/sala-stampa/en/bollettino/pubblico/2017/12/29/171229c.html.

Acknowledgments

The ideas that fertilized this book began in 2015 during my installation as the John Courtney Murray Chair in Public Service. At that time I invited His Eminence Cardinal Gianfranco Ravasi, president of the Pontifical Council for Culture, to participate and be part of an unprecedented colloquium with prominent Latinx theologians titled "The Preferential Option for Culture in Latino/a Theology." During my diplomatic service as US Ambassador to the Holy See (2009–12) I had the opportunity to meet and engage many members of the Roman Curia and meet a number of prominent international theological voices. Among all those I met, I held Cardinal Ravasi in high regard as someone who stood out in Rome as a man of faith with broad intellectual depth, and great openness to engage in dialogue within and outside of the Roman Catholic Church. His groundbreaking initiative, "The Courtyard of the Gentiles," exemplifies these three personal characteristics. My gratitude for this book begins with recognizing Cardinal Ravasi, his contribution to the success of our colloquium, and his willingness to write the foreword to this book.

I also want acknowledge all the scholars that participated in this critical conversation on culture with Ravasi. Their ideas planted the seed that would translate into this book: Maria Teresa Dávila (Merrimack College), "A 'Preferential Option': A Challenge to Faith in a Culture of Privilege"; Neomi De Anda (University of Dayton), "Your *Caridad del Cobre* is not My Guadalupe, but Let's Share La Leche: Expressions of Latino/a Theological Roots in Images of Breast Milk"; Marian K. Díaz (Wisdom Ways Center for Spirituality), "Futuring Our Past: The Origins, Evolutions, and Future of Latino/a Theology"; Orlando O. Espín (University of San Diego), "Popular Catholicism, *sensus fidelium,* and the Faith of the Church"; Roberto S. Goizueta (Boston College), "Jesus, Our Companion"; Néstor Medina (Emmanuel College, University of Toronto), "(De)Ciphering *Mestizaje*: Encrypting Lived Faith"; Carmen Nanko-Fernández (Catholic Theological Union), "Playing en los Márgenes: Lo Popular as *Locus Theologicus*"; and Jean-Pierre Ruiz (St. John's University), "Beyond Borders and Boundaries: Rethinking Eisegesis and Rereading Ruth 1:16–17."

I want to thank the following colleagues from Loyola University Chicago for their generous support: Rev. Michael Garanzini, SJ, past president of Loyola University Chicago, John P. Pelissero, past provost of Loyola University Chicago, Rev. Thomas Regan, past dean of the College of Arts and Sciences. And from the Hank Center at Loyola I want to thank in particular Rev. Mark Bosco, SJ, Michael Murphy, Gabija Steponenaite, John Crowley Buck, Meghan Toomey, and all the graduate and undergraduate assistants who helped me put together this colloquium. I am also very grateful for the support I received from Susan A. Ross, past chair of the theology department, Robert Divito, current chair, and to my colleagues within and outside of the theology department at Loyola University Chicago. Finally, I want to thank my graduate assistants Andy Blosser, Evan Marsolek, Zaccary Haney, and Jack Nuelle for helping me organize and proofread various documents associated with the colloquium and this book.

I also offer my word of gratitude to my Latinx colleagues *en la lucha* from ACHTUS, the Academy of Catholic Hispanic Theologians of the United States, and from the HTI, the Hispanic Theological Initiative. Our work in theological education, like that of my colleagues in the diplomatic corps, serves to build bridges of understanding across cultures and among peoples.

Special word of thanks goes to my friends and colleagues Carmen Nanko-Fernández and Jean-Pierre Ruiz. Beyond their contributions to the colloquium and this volume, they have also helped edit these texts. Our work *en conjunto* has brought us closer together in the service of our Latinx communities. I am grateful to the Catholic Theological Union and their Bechtold Library for providing a welcoming and supportive environment, as well Richard McCarron for his editorial suggestions. I am grateful to Robert Ellsberg, and from Fordham University Press, John Garza and the editorial staff for their support and labors on this book and the Disruptive Cartographers Series.

I want to thank Judith F. Baca, renowned artist, scholar, educator, and activist, for granting me permission to use her mural *Danza de la Tierra* as the cover art for this book. Baca is the co-founder and artistic director of the Social and Public Art Resource Center (SPARC), and her art, work, and commitments address the equality of all persons, the struggle for human rights, and the connections of community to place. I also want to thank the staff of the Dallas Latino Cultural Center, where *Danza de la Tierra* is located, and in particular Benjamin Espino, the General Manager, for their welcome and the opportunity to view the mural.

I want to thank our Latin@ communities, our faith communities, and our families, for inspiring our work and to whom we hold ourselves accountable. I am particularly blessed and grateful to have the unconditional love and support of four amazing children: Josh, Ana, Emmanuel, and Miguel David. Finally, no words can express the gratitude owed to Michael for his unwavering accompaniment.

Miguel H. Díaz

Introduction

A Preferential Option for Culture

Miguel H. Díaz

Ever since Latino/a theology emerged in the early 1970s, Latino/a theologians in the United States have been reflecting on the faith of our people, as practiced and communicated from one generation to another. At the 1995 annual meeting of the Academy of Catholic Hispanic Theologians of the United States (ACHTUS) in New York I raised the following theological question: "What would Catholic systematics look like if it were done *latinamente?*" That question led to the publication of *From the Heart of Our People* (Orbis, 1999). That volume came about as a result of a *teología en conjunto*, a theological methodology well known within Latino/a circles in which Latino/a theologians engage one another in a communal dialogue to explore issues of faith in relationship to their ordinary and daily life experiences (*lo cotidiano*). Reflecting on the faith of Latino/a communities, Orlando O. Espín and I coined the expression "the preferential option for culture" and argued that this option characterizes Latino/a theology.

To be sure, culture does not exist in the abstract; it is a dynamic, complex, historical, and always embodied reality. Oftentimes, when we think of culture, we think of culturally situated persons and their distinct cultural and hybrid identities. As

Kathryn Tanner proposes, cultural identity is "a hybrid, relational affair, something that lives between as much as within cultures."[1] Human experiences related to religion, socioeconomic conditions, political affiliations, gender, sexual orientation, physical ability, and immigration status, to name but a few, often provide the threads that weave together our cultural identities. In our use of the expression "the preferential option for culture" in this volume we more often than not refer to concrete Latino/a persons and the web of human experiences that have shaped their humanity. It is in this way of being human, *latinamente*, in all of its dynamism, fluidity, and complexity, that Latinos/as encounter the life-giving presence of God in history.

On March 26, 2015, I invited a number of prominent voices in Latino/a theology to come to Loyola University Chicago and engage in critical conversation with His Eminence Cardinal Gianfranco Ravasi.[2] This encounter turned out to be an unprecedented moment in the development of Latino/a theologies marked by mutual respect, friendship, and an exchange of ideas with a prominent voice in the Roman Curia. Cardinal Ravasi is the past president of the Pontifical Council for Culture, and widely known as a prolific writer on the Bible and biblical languages. He received international acclaim for his initiative "The Court of the Gentiles." Through this initiative, he has engaged numerous publics in efforts to relate Christian faith with the cultural challenges of our time. This volume reflects the spirit of his groundbreaking initiative to build bridges of understanding among peoples and communities. It seeks a cultural encounter

---

[1] Kathryn Tanner, *Theories of Culture: An Agenda for Theology* (Minneapolis: Fortress Press, 1997), 57–58.

[2] For a summary of the conference and the presenters, see Carmen Nanko-Fernández, "Latin@ Theology and the Preferential Option for Culture," *America* (April 10, 2015), https://www.americamagazine.org/voices/carmen-nanko-fernandez.

between Christian faith and the salient human experiences that map Latino/a communities in the United States.

Rooted in the faith of a people, this volume rethinks theological issues *latinamente* for the sake of contributing to the ongoing development of Christian theological traditions. It places Latino/a theology at the service of the struggle, *la lucha*, to uphold the dignity and fundamental human rights of all the people of God, especially the marginalized, the poor, and the oppressed. Pursuant to this objective, this volume presents theological perspectives that disrupt, as well as envision anew, Christian theological traditions.

As the chapters make evident, Latino/a theology is not a monolithic discipline. Grammatically speaking, theology can always be likened more to a verb than a noun. Latino/a theology certainly reflects this dynamic nature of theology with respect to its theoretical diversity and praxis-oriented methodologies. Thus, while the theological reflections that follow express theology done *latinamente*, the theologians in this volume have unleashed their theological creativity with their own distinctive situated stances, sources, and methodologies. Expressing a sense of oneness through diversity, the authors map their ideas from particular places and tap into sources that constitute the rich landscape of Hispanic Catholicism. Notwithstanding the richness of these theological cartographies, the authors remain committed to doing the kind of theology that emerges *from* and speaks *to* the faith of our people.

Chapter 1 advances some claims related to cultural mediations of the word of God as experienced and interpreted from Latinx perspectives. After focusing on crossing encounters in the Gospel of Mark that are life-giving for Jesus' interlocutors, my chapter explores the *Nican Mopohua* and Nuestra Señora de Guadalupe as another example of the word becoming culture. These initial reflections open the door to further consideration of how this word continues to assume a cultural face resonant with the particularities of peoples, especially those who are marginalized.

Chapter 2 entertains the theme of crossing borders and boundaries from biblical theological perspectives. Jean-Pierre Ruiz creatively rethinks the relationship between exegesis and eisegesis, proposing a bidirectional conversation with Ruth 1:16–17 over issues of identity, connecting, and belonging. His collaborative, connected, and committed strategy of interpretation engages with the world *of* the biblical text and *beyond* the text to include Ruth's twenty-first-century immigrant and refugee *comadres*. The chapter demonstrates the value of "engaging" biblical texts in order to make a difference, hermeneutically and ethically speaking, with respect to contemporary human experiences. Surely, one cannot commend enough this kind of theological effort that seeks to make a difference in a world that Pope Francis has fittingly characterized as exhibiting the globalization of human indifference.

Chapter 3 reflects on the "preferential option for" within the context of privilege and the culture wars in the United States of America. María Teresa Dávila proposes a Latino/a cartographic turn that interrupts and decenters dominant individualistic anthropologies that too often result in violence, arguing instead for a communal anthropology capable of empowering an *option for* the poor, culture, creation. This option for others represents an epistemology and praxis that historicizes Christ's basic teaching to love our neighbors, especially those who are poor, marginalized, and oppressed.

In Chapter 4, Néstor Medina tackles the experience of *mestizaje*, historic and complex experiences of mixture (including biological, racial, and cultural), that has served as a *locus theologicus* for Latino/a theologies. Medina explores the multivalent and complex nature of *mestizaje* and demonstrates its anthropological value with respect to the acts of constituting and claiming human identity. He argues for the theological relevance of *mestizaje*, especially with respect to relating human and divine life as it pertains to Christ and issues of human identity. Chapter 5 concludes this volume, retrieving and turning to las *Cantigas de Santa María*, a thirteenth-century manuscript of poems of Marian devotion that includes the earliest portrayal of a bat and ball game in the Iberian Peninsula. Carmen Nanko-Fernández breaks new theological ground in her option for culture as she "plays" theologically on the margins of sport and theology. Her constructive theological interpretation of Cantiga 42 explores not only the good life that sport may foster, but more important, the interrelationship and fluidity that characterizes *lo popular* at the intersections of popular Catholicism and popular culture. "Playing" within and outside the fields that shape our daily Latin@ living (*lo cotidiano*) has ancient roots and sources too often neglected in contemporary constructive theologies.

This volume lifts up the distinct cultural experiences of Latinas/os as an act of resistance against human indifference and in defense of the human dignity of all persons. Pope Francis rightly observes that "theology must address conflicts: not only those that we experience within the Church, but also those that concern the world as a whole and those which are lived on the streets."[3] Echoing Thomas Aquinas's central teaching that grace presupposes and builds upon nature, the pope asserts that "grace presupposes culture, and God's gift becomes flesh in the culture of those who receive it."[4] The authors in this volume have opted for the "streets"

---

[3] Pope Francis, "Letter to the Grand Chancellor of the Catholic University of Argentina," March 3, 2015, https://w2.vatican.va/content/francesco/en/letters/2015/documents/papa-francesco_20150303_lettera-universita-cattolica-argentina.html.

[4] Pope Francis, *Evangelii Gaudium*, ¶115, November 24, 2013, http://www.vatican.va/content/francesco/en/apost_exhortations/documents/papa-francesco_esortazione-ap_20131124_evangelii-gaudium.html. On Aquinas, see "gratia non tollit naturam, sed perficit," *Summa Theologiae* (*ST*),

as geographical places, past and present, where we presuppose the experience of grace and encounter with God. As Cardinal Ravasi makes clear in the foreword to this volume, because the Word has become flesh, it is quite fitting to continue to search for this Word in human experiences and thereby speak not only of the past becoming the Word in history but also of the present and ethical challenges posed by this becoming within the particularity of diverse cultural experiences. Indeed, to do so is to take seriously the fact that God crossed over into our cultural experiences, so that we could cross over into God's world. Or simply put, the Word of God becomes flesh, so that the flesh can become Word.[5]

I, I, 8 ad 2.

[5] See Jean-Pierre Ruiz, "The Word Became Flesh and the Flesh Becomes Word: Notes toward a US Latino/a Theology of Revelation," in *Building Bridges, Doing Justice: Constructing a Latino/a Ecumenical Theology*, ed. Orlando O. Espín (Maryknoll, NY: Orbis Books, 1970), 47–68.

FOREWORD

Cardinal Gianfranco Ravasi

To understand fully the theological contributions that follow requires a rather ample and articulated premise. Biblical Revelation, in fact, cannot be compared to a sacred meteorite that has fallen into the immanence of the earth and history from the transcendence of the sky. It is, rather, an encounter that turns into an embrace, succinctly described in the famous Johannine assertion *ho Logos sarx egheneto* (Jn 1:14). The divine *Logos* "becomes" human *sarx* in the one person of Christ in whom two natures coexist, the human and the divine.

The Incarnation is the ultimate goal of the process inherent in the totality of biblical Revelation and the history of salvation. In fact, God-Emmanuel and his word meet and express themselves through a continuous dialogue with human cultures. This dialogue moves from the nomadic (think of Easter, a primordial pastoral rite reinterpreted and put into a historical context) to the Phoenician-Canaanite (the demythologized reinterpretation of nuptial symbolism). It moves from the Mesopotamian (the cosmological system) to the Egyptian (the personification of the divine word in the theology of Memphis). It likewise moves from the Hittite (the model of the covenant) to the Persian (the reformulation of eschatology) and the Greek-Hellenic with a wide variety of influences. The New Testament reflects the dialogue between Palestinian Judaism and that of the Diaspora, as well as with Greco-Roman civilization and even some pagan cultural forms.

St. John Paul II, in 1979, stated to the Pontifical Biblical Commission that even before becoming flesh in Jesus Christ, "the same divine Word had previously become human language, assuming the ways of expression of the different cultures which, from Abraham to the seer of the Apocalypse, offered the revered mystery of God's salvific love the possibility of becoming accessible and understandable for successive generations, despite the multiple diversity of their historical situations."[1] The same experience of fruitful osmosis between early Christianity and the cultures of that time was repeated later, becoming a constant in the Christian tradition, beginning with the Fathers of the Church. Suffice it to quote a passage from the second-century *First Apology* of St. Justin the Martyr: "We have been taught that Christ is the first-born of God, and we have declared above that He is the Word of God of whom every race of men were partakers; and those who lived reasonably are Christians, even though they have been taught atheists; as, among the Greeks, Socrates and Heraclitus, and men like them" (46:2–3).[2]

This phenomenon of inculturation sustains Christianity as it encounters the thought, art, and society where it becomes enmeshed. Symbolically this is formulated in the three Gospel metaphors of salt in food (Mt 5:13), leaven in dough (Mt 13:33), and the seed in the ground (Jn 12:24). The category of *synkatabasis*, in Latin *condescensio*, "condescension, adaptation," known already to the Greek and

---

[1] John Paul II, "Address to Members of the Pontifical Biblical Commission," April 26, 1979, http://www.vatican.va/content/john-paul-ii/en/speeches/1979/april/documents/hf_jp-ii_spe_19790426_pont-com-biblica.html.

[2] Justin Martyr, *The First and Second Apologies*, trans. Leslie William Barnard (Mahwah, NJ: Paulist Press, 1997), 55.

Judeo-Hellenistic culture—for example, in Epictetus (*Discourses*, 3, 16, 1–3) and Philo, who uses the angelic ladder of the dream of Jacob (Gn 28:12–13; cf. *De Somniis* 1, 147)—was adopted by Christian theology, from Clement of Alexandria (*Stromata* 7, 9) through to the Second Vatican Council using the Latin term *adaptatio-accomodatio* (*Ad Gentes*, no. 22).[3]

The word and concept "inculturation," which is complex in its specific theological expression and in its concrete pastoral implementation, appears for the first time in a church document in the *Message to the People of God* of the Synod of Bishops of 1977 (no. 5).[4] It received a significant definition in a speech that St. John Paul II addressed to the bishops of Kenya during his trip to Africa in May 1980: "The 'acculturation' or 'inculturation' which you rightly promote will truly be a reflection of the Incarnation of the Word, when a culture, transformed and regenerated by the Gospel, brings forth from its own living tradition original expressions of Christian life, celebration and thought."[5] In this perspective one could freely transcribe the quoted assertion of John 1:14 in this way: "The Word became culture." And if we wanted to substantiate this statement in Christological terms only, we could use the figure of the historical Jesus who reveals his *sarx*, that is, his humanity, in a well-defined culture, and in a manner that does not oppose but integrates with the Christ of faith.

In him the *Logos* becomes, in fact, a Semite, not a Greek, indeed, more precisely, a Hebrew or better a Jew (cf. Jn 4:22 and 19:21),

---

[3] *Decretum de Activitate Missionali Ecclesiae: Ad Gentes*, December 7, 1965, no. 22, http://www.vatican.va/archive/hist_councils/ii_vatican_council/documents/vat-ii_decree_19651207_ad-gentes_en.html.

[4] Messaggio Sinodo dei vescovi," Rome, October 28, 1977, http://www.synod.va/content/synod/en/synodal_assemblies/1977-fourth-ordinary-general-assembly--catechesis-in-our-time.html.

[5] John Paul II, "Address to the Bishops of Kenya," May 7, 1980, no. 6, http://www.vatican.va/content/john-paul-ii/en/speeches/1980/may/documents/hf_jp-ii_spe_19800507_vescovi-kenya.html.

conditioned by a precise historical identity. Jesus is born in a period of national independence for Israel under King Herod the Great, but he is also simultaneously a subject of imperial Rome, as is shown by the census of Quirinius (Lk 2:1–2; cf. 3:1–2). He lives in a limited geographical area, first in Galilee, then Judea, works as a carpenter, becomes an itinerant preacher. He was neither an aristocrat nor a priest, nor an ascetic, nor an Essene in the model of the Baptist. He dies under the Roman governor Pontius Pilate around the year 30 CE. He is, therefore, enclosed in a civilization with historical-spatial and sociocultural coordinates that are well defined, as has been set out in recent decades by the so-called Third Quest.

Jesus Christ, therefore, has a *mind-set* different from that of an Athenian philosopher or many later Fathers of the Church. His thinking and his language proceed symbolically and not analytically, as attested by his *lóghia* and his parables, which are methodologically very different from the reasoning of a Plato or an Aristotle, and also from the assertions of the Councils of Nicaea and Chalcedon. The heart of his message, the Kingdom of God, can be understood only through the monarchies of the ancient Near East, although he will give it a radical conceptual reworking (the "Render to Caesar . . . and to God . . ." in Matthew 22:21) and a concrete originality in the preferential option for the poor.

Now, this very expression typical of Latin American theology—on the basis of what has been said so far—can be rewritten correctly and globally as a "preferential option for culture." It is natural to assume that we use the term "culture" in its current general anthropological sense. In the original term—coined in eighteenth-century Germany (*Kultur*) on the basis of Latin, especially by the man of letters Johann Gottfried Herder—there was an aristocratic angle of understanding. It referred, in fact, only to the so-called high intellectual dimensions, as found in the arts, sciences, philosophy, unlike the use of the word "culture" by Cicero, where he referred to agriculture, even if as a metaphor for the philosophical education of the person.[6]

Within contemporary times we approach, however, more closely, two other classic categories, Greek *paideia* and Latin *humanitas*, which see culture as a civilization and the complete formation of men and women in their historical-geographical context. In practice, "culture" in contemporary understandings embraces the general horizon of human thought and action, recognizing thereby that each subjective and objective, creative and productive process and project, when endowed with its own coherence and meaning, can have "cultural" dignity.

The theological perspective that has just been presented above situates the angle of vision from which to read the various chapters that follow and the contributions they seek to offer to theological research. In this sense, Miguel H. Díaz offers foundational considerations, structural and theological in nature. They emphasize the reciprocal "crossing" between God and humanity, especially in boundary situations, particularly highlighted within Latino/a Catholicism. As he affirms:

> For Latinos/as, the God of Jesus Christ is a God who crosses a dangerous border, experiences the cross as a result of sin and human injustice, and stands in solidarity with those who undertake similar border-crossings. God crosses from divine life to human life undertaking a risky migration for the sake of life. God continues to stand in solidarity with all who risk and hope for the promise of new life, already fulfilled in the resurrection of Christ.[7]

---

[6] Marcus Tullius Cicero, *Tusculanae Disputationes,* Liber 2, #13 (CreateSpace Independent Publishing Platform, 2014), 40.

[7] Miguel H. Díaz, Chapter 1, page 5, of this volume.

In this light, his proposal also justifies the existence of contextual theologies characterized by "the preferential option for culture" in North America and elsewhere in the English-speaking world. At a more general level, this can be associated with a category dear to Latino/a theology, that of the use of *lo cotidiano* as a privileged place for the crossings and epiphanies of God.

Continuing to unfold the notion of the arrival of the divine "beyond borders and boundaries" and also with the realism of human history is the rereading of the passage of Ruth 1:16–17 by Jean-Pierre Ruiz. His contribution follows the rules of doing hermeneutics *latinamente.* The proposed interpretive trilogy—of "collaboration" (*teología de conjunto*), "connection" (*la vida cotidiana*), and "commitment" (in practice the reactualization of the biblical text in new sociocultural contexts)—allows the development of a suggestive profile of Ruth as a foreigner, a righteous proselyte, and a daughter (2:8, 2:22). Ruiz's proposal as a whole thus becomes an invitation to integrate traditional exegetical methods with the contribution of a Latino/a approach that can introduce new dimensions that may be fruitful and dynamic for the study and proclamation of God's Word.

In this very consistent and suggestive itinerary that the sequence of voices in this collection proposes, two significant, and in some ways even provocative stages, are seen in the chapters by María Teresa Dávila and Néstor Medina. In keeping with the spatial metaphor, we can affirm that a cartographic repositioning is at the heart of Dávila's effort that seeks to decentralize *latinamente* by turning to one of the Christian theological categories of the last century, the *preferential option* for others. She places the notion of the person-in-community as part of a necessary cultural shift required to move away from the individualist, hypercapitalist heritage of US Christianity. The turn from individualism to *nosotros*, which can embrace all of creation, starts in the holy, daily messiness of the existential peripheries and encounters the vulnerabilities of others as if they were our own. Such *acompañamiento* would also kill off the so-called culture wars at their very root by eradicating prevailing tendencies to define one's own cause violently over against another's dignity. Dávila's is a religious proposal that has, however, clear and ethical-social consequences capable of inserting itself into the current coordinates of an aggressive society and politics.

With a different approach, but following a similar itinerary, Néstor Medina centers his proposal on an anthropological-sociological and religious-moral notion that has received much attention and close interest in recent years, namely, *mestizaje*. From a concept that was held in some disdain, articulated in such terms as "mongrel, half-breed, half-blood, mulatto, mixed race," *mestizaje* has been transformed into a positive cultural and spiritual dialogical vision. Medina notes that if the banner *cogito ergo sum* symbolizes the West as influenced by the Enlightenment, *nosotros existimos y vivimos* defines well the world of *mestizaje*, a vital experience for Latino/as, some 20 percent of the US population and among Catholics, the fastest-growing group. The category and condition of *mestizaje* is not just biological. It draws on the historical intermixture of indigenous communities with the Spanish and Portuguese colonialists but also has an unsettled and unsettling nature. The fluid "in-between identity" of Latinas/os is disruptive of the pretended securities of dominant culture. So it is often an unwelcome cultural tradition in the United States because it reveals cultural assimilationist and colonizing social and religious attitudes.

By adopting *mestizaje* as a theological vantage point and culture as a fundamental *locus theologicus*, new ways of thinking theologically about faith experience are unlocked. Far from simply celebrating a romanticized ethno-cultural group, it forces a complexifying revision of history. For Medina, this allows a new vision of humanity and of Christianity: Jesus is reclaimed as *mestizo,* precisely because his mixing is of the divine and the human. His life and message is *mestizizing,* in that it breaks down cultural, racial, and ethnic barriers, bringing people, peoples, and cultures together to see their divine image and attain their full humanity while remembering their violent history. It also dissipates the ideal of a universal human and grounds what it means to be human in the detail, the accidental, and the particularity of experience. As theological reflections are shaped and conditioned by experience *en y de conjunto* (from within the community and belonging to the community), then the indigenous, African, and Latin American intellectual reservoirs, which do not appeal directly to the Enlightenment, can offer new—and grounded—epistemologies for theology.

Finally, the proposal offered by Carmen Nanko-Fernández, which adopts a category well accepted even by the apostle Paul, that of sport (cf. 1 Cor 9:24–27; 2 Tm 4:7–8), is thought-provoking. Her reference—albeit critical—is oriented toward baseball, a typical US sport, which is then taken as a metaphor of existence and daily experience using a free "allegorical" analysis both of Cantiga 42 of the *Cantigas de Santa Maria* of Alfonso X and of the image of what might be Madonna of Essen depicted in the accompanying panel of illustrations. Similarly, in this case, *lo cotidiano* features as a *locus theologicus,* with all the complexity that the "incarnation" in a similar popular reality reveals, both in a positive and limited sense, and even in certain negative aspects, that the experience involves.

The chapters constituting this volume are gathered inclusively in a sort of rainbow of many colors, all coherent and harmonic. The thread of light holding them together is that radical Christian truth from which we started, the Incarnation, that is to say, the intimate and deep weaving between *Logos* and *sarx,* between eternity and history, between transcendence and immanence. Certainly, as the Christological controversies of the early centuries show, the equilibrium that needs to be observed is similar to a mountain ridge, a cutting space that unites the two sides and on which it is difficult to proceed. From our side, anyhow, we reiterate the interest that these contributions in Latino/a theology can create in contemporary theology. At a more general level, they express an awareness of the need for an encounter of the Christian faith with contemporary culture in the diverse multiplicity of its expressions.

1

THE WORD THAT CROSSES

Life-Giving Encounters
with the Markan Jesus and Guadalupe

Miguel H. Díaz

Central to the Christian doctrine of God is the fundamental revelation that God has crossed into history for our sake and our salvation. Contemporary Christian theologians have distanced themselves from ahistorical and abstract theologizing, drawing instead from the rich biblical notion of a God who walks with and relates to concrete persons. As Walter Kasper observes, "The Christian's concern is not with God in himself but with God-for-us, the God of Jesus Christ, who is a God of human beings (Heb. 11.16)."[1] Christian belief names this divine revelation Emmanuel—a name that suggests God's personal and life-giving interactions.[2] Unlike

---

[1] Walter Kasper, *The God of Jesus Christ* (New York: Crossroad, 1989), 158.

[2] Theologians have noted that the revelation of God's name to Moses in Exodus 3:14 invites us to consider the personal and dynamic nature of God and God's promise to remain a permanent presence in history. John Courtney Murray, for instance, renders the following translation and interpretation of the divine name: "I will be there as who I am will I be there" (Ex 3:14). See John Courtney Murray, *The Problem of God* (New Haven, CT: Yale University Press, 1964), 10.

the philosopher's "Unmoved Mover," Scripture and tradition give witness to this personal God, who moves within and is moved by human persons, especially in their histories of suffering and marginalization.[3]

The documents of the Second Vatican Council invite us to consider that revelation is concerned with the sharing of God's life. But divine life is always expressed through human experiences and culturally mediated words. Religious texts such as the Bible, and other texts produced within Christian theological traditions, seek to capture the essence of this revelation.[4] While the Bible serves as a privileged cultural text of God's revelation within Christian tradition, it is not the only source providing insight into God's life-giving encounters in history.

The expression "the word that crosses" used in the title of this chapter fittingly points to the encounter between God and humanity. It invites us to consider that in revelation two things come together: God's self-communication and the human as the recipient of that communication. On the one hand, we know that God is beyond materiality, cannot be confined to space and time. On the other hand, we also know that persons communicate with God in embodied and contextual ways. Thus the expression "the word that crosses" metaphorically suggests the myriad ways we *humanly* experience, name, and interpret the presence of God in history. Jesus, as Word made flesh, is culturally bound, and his words are connected to his human history. So too are all subsequent discernments and interpretations of God's self-communication.

Discussing the nature of revelation, the Dogmatic Constitution on Divine Revelation observes that both Scripture and

---

[3] See John Zizioulas, *Being as Communion, Studies in Personhood and the Church* (New York: St. Vladimir's Seminary Press, 1985), 15–66.

[4] See Orlando O. Espín, *Idol and Grace: On Traditioning and Subversive Hope* (Maryknoll, NY: Orbis Books, 2014), 39–75.

tradition have the same "wellspring" (*Dei Verbum*, 9). Both serve
as loci for God's self-communication. Both express the divine presence in history through human words. Sandra Schneiders rightly
cautions, however, that we should not make the mistake of understanding all the words of the Bible simply as revelation. What
she argues with respect to the interpretation of the Bible equally
applies, mutatis mutandis, to discerning the revelatory character of
any other culturally situated words that seek to communicate God's
life-giving encounters in history:

> The referent of the metaphor "word of God" is, then, a
> complex reality much broader than the written scrip-
> tures. . . . Just as we must say that sacred scripture is (and
> is not) the word of God, so we cannot say that the Bible
> is, purely and simply, revelation. It is more correct to say
> that the Bible is (potentially) revelatory than to say that it
> is revelation. Scripture is a privileged witness to the divine
> self-gift that has been taking place from the moment of
> creation and will continue until the end of time. But it
> is symbolic witness, and that means that it becomes the
> actual locus of divine-human encounter only in the act
> of interpretation. This interpretation becomes an arduous
> task because symbols are inherently and invincibly ambig-
> uous, simultaneously revealing and concealing.[5]

Theology partly entails wrestling with how Scripture and other
culturally situated texts reveal God's life-giving encounters with
creation. Mindful of Schneiders's invitation to wrestle with the
"word of God" and interpret its revelatory potential, this chapter
makes some claims related to cultural mediations of this word in

---

[5] Sandra M. Schneiders, *The Revelatory Text: Interpreting the New Testament as Sacred Scripture* (Collegeville, MN: Liturgical Press, 1999), 39.

the Markan Jesus and in Guadalupe. The chapter is organized into
three sections that explore the theme of cultural mediations of the
word of God. The Gospel of Mark, a text that rose within colonial Roman occupation, speaks of God crossing into marginalized
Jewish and gentile communities in the person of Jesus of Nazareth.
The *Nican Mopohua*, a text that rose within colonial Spanish occupation, speaks of Guadalupe, God's agent, crossing into indigenous
and marginalized communities that suffered the consequences
of this occupation.[6] These two texts provide windows into God's
self-revelation during times of communal oppression, cultural
suppression, and imperial rule. Each offers us the possibility of
tapping into vernacular translations of original texts that depend
on hermeneutically contested religious expressions. These texts
provide rich theological sources to consider God's self-communication in history.[7] As a way to transition from life-giving crossings in
the Gospel of Mark to life-giving crossings in the *Nican Mopohua*,
I will offer some theological reflections grounded in the scholar-

---

[6] On the *Nican Mopohua,* see Virgilio Elizondo, *Guadalupe: Mother
of New Creation* (Maryknoll, NY: Orbis Books, 1997), 5–22. All quotes in
this chapter will be taken from Elizondo's own English translation based
on a Spanish translation by Clodomiro Siller Acuña. I recognize the limitations of depending on translations; however, the Elizondo translation is
widely used and recognizable in Latino/a theologies. Please note that the
numbers referencing texts in the *Nican Mopohua* found in the subheadings
of this chapter are drawn from the Elizondo translation (other translations
may vary). Passages quoted within the body of this chapter will be cited
according to the page they appear on in the Elizondo *Guadalupe* book. For
the text in Náhuatl with an English translation, see "Nican Mopohua: Here
It Is Told," January 20, 2019, University of California San Diego, https://
pages.ucsd.edu/~dkjordan/nahuatl/nican/nican1.html. For translations
in multiple languages, see José Luis G. Guerrero, *El Nican Mopohua: Un
intento de exegesis* (Mexico City: Universidad Pontificia de México, 1996).

[7] On the Gospel of Mark, see *The Gospel of Mark: A Social-Rhetor-
ical Commentary* (Grand Rapids, MI: Wm. Eerdmans, 2001). On *Nican
Mopohua,* see Guerrero, *El Nican Mopohua.*

ship of Karl Rahner. These reflections explore fundamental issues related to the revelatory character of human encounters with God and the cultural mediations of those encounters. This theological exploration into a word that crosses for the sake of life-giving encounters can be summarized *latinamente* as follows: For Latinos/as, the God of Jesus Christ is a God who crosses a dangerous border, experiences the cross as a result of sin and human injustice, and stands in solidarity with those who undertake similar border-crossings. God crosses from divine life to human life undertaking a risky migration for the sake of life. God continues to stand in solidarity with all who risk and hope for the promise of new life, already fulfilled in the resurrection of Christ. In continuity with Christian theological voices from diverse backgrounds and philosophical traditions of the past, Latinx theology affirms that in Jesus Christ, God has been revealed as a God who is *for-us*. And similar to the central claim made in Latin American liberation theology, Latinx theologies of God seek to probe "the triune life itself, however mediated, incarnated, and historicized."[8] Or simply put: Latinx theologies also invite us to consider the word that crosses to become culture.

Crossings in the Gospel of Mark

Scholars disagree with respect to the date, communal origins, and time of the composition of the Gospel of Mark.[9] Many, however, agree that given its theology, which highlights Jesus as

---

[8] Ignacio Ellacuría, "The Historicity of Christian Salvation," in *Mysterium Liberationis: Fundamental Concepts of Liberation Theology*, ed. Ignacio Ellacuría and Jon Sobrino (Maryknoll, NY: Orbis Books, 1993), 277.

[9] David E. Garland, *A Theology of Mark's Gospel*, ed. Andreas J. Köstenberger (Grand Rapids, MI: Zondervan, 2015). See also Pheme Perkins, "Mark: Jesus, Suffering Messiah," in *Reading the New Testament* (New York: Paulist Press, 1978), 203–13.

suffering messiah, this gospel likely emerged around the time of the Jewish revolt against Rome and the destruction of the Temple (70 CE). "One can infer from the prominence given to the issue of persecution in Mark that the gospel was composed in a context where being a follower of Jesus was laden with danger."[10]

Be that as it may, the Gospel of Mark often depicts Jesus as an outsider who participates in various life-giving encounters. This status of Jesus as an outsider is complex and fluid, as seen in Jesus' interactions with a variety of characters that belong to different groups. Mark presents Jesus as the agent of God who moves within various landscapes and among persons who often do not share his religious, cultural, or sociopolitical traditions. In Mark's Gospel, the outsiders, rather than Jesus' inner circle of disciples (4:13, 6:52, 7:18, 8:21), are more likely to identify Jesus as the suffering messiah. For instance, at the crucifixion, it is the Roman centurion who identifies Jesus as Son of God in his condition of vulnerability and suffering (15:39).

One possible interpretation of Mark's story of Jesus would be to see it as a tale of borders and boundary crossings. From this perspective Jesus is someone who engages in various geographical and cultural crossings. These crossings offer clues into the life-giving presence of God in history. In the cases of Mark 5:1–20 and Mark 7:24–37, Jesus ventures outside of Judea and Galilee, into lands not his own. In the raising of Jairus's daughter (5:21–24, 35–43), Jesus reaches across the boundary between life and death. But Jesus is not the only one doing the crossing. In Mark 5:25–34, for instance, the hemorrhaging woman who touches Jesus transgresses the boundaries of decorum. These narratives of crossings all share the motif of life, and of human words and actions associated with life.

---

[10] Garland, *A Theology of Mark's Gospel*, 68.

The Exorcism of the Gerasene Demoniac (Mark 5:1–20)

Jesus crosses the Sea of Galilee and enters the largely gentile territory of the Gerasenes in the region of the Decapolis (5:1), where he encounters a man possessed by a spirit who identifies as "Legion, for we are many" (5:9). There, Jesus performs an exorcism on one who was probably not a Jew, by allowing unclean spirits to enter a herd of swine feeding on the hillside. The biblical text indicates that Jesus is operating in a cultural and religious milieu different from his own. That pigs were in the area further implies that Jesus was not in a predominantly Jewish territory.

How physical illness often relates to personal isolation and social marginalization in the gospels and how Jesus' words and actions affect these conditions have been widely studied. Of particular interest are the interpretations that come from psychosocial points of view.[11] With respect to the latter, the life-giving encounter between Jesus and the Gerasene man serves as a test case for the kind of displacement that persons experienced during Roman occupation, the communal fears faced by occupied communities. In this sense, some scholars argue that the stories about demonic possessions can be interpreted as manifesting, objectifying, and naming oppressive human conditions under the Roman Empire. For instance, some suggest that the word "Legion," the name the Gerasene uses to identify himself, hints at the sociopsychological illness of persons that Roman occupation produced: "For this demoniac is able to 'give the Romans the devil' by identifying their legions, probably the most visible Roman presence to him, with demons. However, he is able to do that only obliquely, through madness."[12]

---

[11] For instance, see Paul W. Hollenbach, "Jesus, Demoniacs, and Public Authorities: A Socio-Historical Study," *Journal of the American Academy of Religion* 49, no. 4 (1981): 567–88.

[12] Hollenbach, "Jesus," 581.

As is often the case, psychological and social oppression produces communal isolation, a displacement from human relations that marginalizes persons and for all practical purposes no longer considers them to be among the living: "He lived among the tombs and no one could restrain him anymore, even with chains" (5:3). Jesus recognizes this human condition of the Gerasene and permits the spirits to leave him and enter the pigs. Perhaps the community's reaction to the healing performed by Jesus reveals the social fears brought about by Roman occupation and the communal danger posed by anyone who dared to challenge the status quo. Instead of finding comfort in the actions of Jesus, the community expresses fear and begs him to leave (5:17).

In this story Jesus' crossing yields life in the form of personal empowerment. As a result of his healing, the Gerasene moves from a place where he was treated as if he were dead to a place where he could proclaim the life-giving power of God: "And he went away and began to proclaim in the Decapolis how much Jesus had done for him; and everyone was amazed" (5:20). In effect, the healing renders this man socially visible by restoring his human agency and re-incorporating him into communal relationships. This life-giving encounter, with all the physical and social implications implied, can be summarized as follows:

> Jesus' disruption of the prevailing accommodation is indicated especially by one of the more puzzling aspects of the story, namely, the fear of some of the townspeople, which is manifested in their request to Jesus that he go out of their neighborhood. Perhaps we can account for this response, which seems not to be directly connected to the loss of the 2,000 swine (or is it another slur on the legions? "They are swine!"), by suggesting that Jesus' healing of the demoniac brought the man's and the neighborhood's hatred of the Romans out in the open, where the result

could be disaster for the community. The man evidently was a loudmouth (Mark 5:20), which made his healing doubly dangerous. . . . Jesus appears as an outside trouble-maker whom the locals wish would get out of town and never show up again.[13]

The Restoration of Jairus's Daughter (Mark 5:21–24, 35–43)
and the Healing of the Hemorrhaging Woman (Mark 5:25–34)

Next in this series of stories we find Jesus crossing again "in the boat to the other side" (5:21). Jesus is not the only one crossing borders and social boundaries in these two life-giving stories that take place in this region.

Jairus, a synagogue official, comes to Jesus and appeals for his help to heal his dying daughter. The flow of this narrative is interrupted by another life-giving encounter, this time with a hemorrhaging woman. This literary technique of pausing an action is used in other parts of this gospel (e.g., 11:12–21). It offers Mark the opportunity to invite readers to enter into a kind of literary limbo. This ploy builds suspense. In the case of Jairus's daughter, it leaves the audience perplexed by Jesus' failure to promptly address her imminent life-threatening condition.

Mark embeds another narrative, the interaction with a hemor-rhaging woman who approaches Jesus from behind and touches his cloak (5:27–28). This "touch" is significant because the woman takes the initiative to cross boundaries dealing with gender and decorum.

Jesus acknowledges the woman's norm-defying behavior and calls it faith (Mark 5:34). He addresses her as "Daughter" and in this way grants her a new status. She is daughter within a new *familia dei*. The healing of the woman suffering from hemorrhages means (for the

---

[13] Hollenbach, "Jesus," 581.

moment) the death of Jairus's daughter and puts them both in deadly competition with one another.[14]

The Gospel of Mark then proceeds to end the literary limbo left with the unresolved situation surrounding the daughter of Jairus. Her illness has in fact resulted in physical death: While Jesus "was still speaking" to the healed woman, "some people came from the leader's house to say, 'Your daughter is dead. Why trouble the teacher any further?'" (5:35). But the news of her death does not stop Jesus from responding. The power of God's life knows no borders. Mark tells us that Jesus, driven by faith, rather than fear, heads for Jairus's house (5:36–37).

Before entering the house, Jesus sends "all outside" (5:40) and brings inside the parents and those who were with him. Note here the insider/outsider motif characteristic of this gospel as Jesus sends the mourners out of the house, those who, in the moment, could not imagine the possibility of life. After their removal, Jesus then takes the child by the hand and tells her, "*Talitha koum*," which means, "Little girl, I say to you, arise" (5:41). Through the raising of Jairus's daughter, Jesus demonstrates the power of God's word to cross the boundary between death and life.

The Healing of the Daughter of the Syrophoenician Woman (Mark 7:24–37)

The story of Jesus' interaction with the Syrophoenician woman offers another valuable biblical window into Jesus' geocultural movements. From the perspective of Jesus, the itin-

---

[14] Monika Fander, "Gospel of Mark: Women as True Disciples of Jesus," in *Feminist Biblical Interpretation: A Compendium of Critical Commentary on the Books of the Bible and Related Literature,* ed. Luise Schottroff and Marie-Theres Wacker (Grand Rapids, MI: William B. Eerdmans, 2012), 631.

erant visitor to the gentile city of Tyre, the Syrophoenician is
an outsider, but from the perspective of the woman, Jesus is the
stranger in her land. "By making his way into the region of Tyre,
he finds himself in a location where he is *other* in multiple ways to
the dominant sectors of society and to his Syrophoenician interlocutor in particular."[15]

The Syrophoenician woman comes to Jesus begging him to
cast a demon out of her daughter. Jesus' reply is shocking. Instead
of responding to the woman's needs with compassion, Jesus offers
a sharp reprimand: "Let the children be fed first, for it is not fair to
take the children's food and throw it to the dogs" (7:27). But the
gentile woman, the first person in the Gospel of Mark to call Jesus
"Lord," will not be silenced by his response, nor will she give up on
her desire to see her daughter healed. She quickly rises to the occasion and challenges Jesus: "Sir, even the dogs under the table eat
the children's crumbs" (7:28). Her persistence and wisdom prompt
Jesus to reverse his initial response and address the life-threatening
experience that her daughter faces.

Some traditional interpretations of this text have highlighted
how this episode contrasts with the story that immediately
precedes it (7:1–23), comparing and contrasting the interactions
between Jesus and the Syrophoenician woman with Jesus' interactions with the disciples, insiders who lack understanding. Such a
line of interpretation focuses on how this woman pushes Jesus to
transcend the particularity of his Jewish background. In this sense,
the Syrophoenician woman enables Jesus to become more mindful
of his catholic mission. In other words, as a result of interacting
with this outsider, Jesus realizes that he is not simply a Jew called
to serve the house of Israel but a child of God called to serve God's
family, a social body that knows no borders. Although this interpretative

---

[15] Jean-Pierre Ruiz, *Readings from the Edges: The Bible and People on
the Move* (Maryknoll, NY: Orbis Books, 2011), 49.

approach carries some value, Jesus' interaction with this woman can also prompt another angle of interpretation, especially one more in line with this chapter.

With respect to Jesus' harsh response to this woman's original request, various explanations have been offered. Among these, consider the following. Jesus at first refuses to adhere to her request because he identifies the woman with a people who may have disproportionately shared and exploited the region's resources.[16] In this sense, Jesus would appear to take the side of the marginalized by denouncing the powerful. But note how in the woman's words to him ("Sir, even the dogs under the table eat the children's crumbs") she "relinquishes the place of privilege his response attributes to her."[17] Once again, using a literary technique to convey meaning, the "words" this woman speaks to Jesus "move" her into a place of vulnerability, a place where she can receive only what is left over for those displaced from human households.[18] And as Jean-Pierre Ruiz observes, "It is 'because of this word' of hers (Mark 7:29) that Jesus accedes to her request—performing what is in Mark's Gospel *the only healing miracle that does not involve a face-to-face encounter* between Jesus and the one in need of the healing."[19] While the uncharitable nature of Jesus' harsh response to this woman cannot be explained away, this woman's words provoke a change in Jesus.[20]

---

[16] See Sharon H. Ringe, "A Gentile Woman's Story," in *Feminist Interpretation of the Bible,* ed. Letty M. Russell (Philadelphia: Westminster, 1985), 65–72. See also Ruiz's *Reading from the Edges,* 44–50.

[17] Sharon H. Ringe, "A Gentile Woman's Story, Revisited: Rereading Mark 7.24–31," in *Feminist Companion to Mark,* ed. A. J. Levine and M. Blickenstaff (Sheffield, UK: Sheffield Academic Press, 2001), 90. Also cited in Ruiz, *Reading from the Edges,* 47.

[18] Ringe, "A Gentile Woman's Story, Revisited," 90. See also Ruiz, *Readings from the Edges,* 48.

[19] Ruiz, *Reading from the Edges,* 48. Emphasis added.

[20] See Ruiz, *Reading from the Edges,* 46.

This gospel story and the stories of the Gerasene, Jairus's daughter, and the hemorrhaging woman are not the only sources that can be tapped within the Bible or within various Christian traditions to support the notion of a God whose life-giving word crosses to give life. In a similar way, the *Nican Mopohua* also witnesses the life-giving encounter of a word that comes from God, crosses, and becomes culture.

Theological Foundations:
The Word Crosses into Culture

Karl Rahner offers a theological foundation to understand how the life-giving crossing of the word of God in Christ and witnessed in the Bible can be related to the ongoing and life-giving crossing of this word with respect to other culturally situated texts such as the *Nican Mopohua*. The metaphor "hearer of the Word" summarizes Rahner's theological anthropology.[21] This metaphor draws from his profoundly sacramental approach to human history, a history that Rahner interprets to be ontologically graced and Christologically oriented.[22] Rahner argues that the human person

---

[21] See Karl Rahner, *Hearer of the Word*, trans. Joseph Donceel (New York: Continuum, 1994).

[22] Rahner sees Christ as the ontological cause and end of all that exists. The following often-cited quote summarizes his theological anthropology and his view of the potential revelatory character of our historical efforts to encounter the life of God: "Because it is the union of the real essence of God and of man in God's personal self-expression in his eternal Logos, for this reason Christology is the beginning and the end of anthropology, and this anthropology in its most radical actualization is for all eternity theology. It is first of all the theology which God himself has spoken by uttering his Word as our flesh into the emptiness of what is not God and is even sinful, and secondly, it is the theology which we ourselves do in faith when we do not think that we could find Christ by going around man, and hence find God by going around the human altogether." See Karl Rahner,

is spirit in the world, and as such, history, the body, and the senses
are indispensable elements that mediate the human encounter with
God. Influenced by Thomas Aquinas's theological anthropology
and epistemology, Rahner affirms the incarnational nature of our
encounter with God.[23] Human persons, argues Rahner, are on the
lookout to hear the word of God, seeking the revelation of this
word within the ordinariness of their life experiences.[24] Rahner
points out that "if this revelation has to come in human history, if
it comes at all . . . if we are from the start referred to history, within
which this revelation may possibly come, then we are essentially the
beings who, in our innermost nature, *listen to a possible revelation of
God through the word in human history*."[25]

It is beyond the scope of this chapter to explore in depth
the implications of Rahner's transcendental anthropology for a
theology of revelation. Suffice it to say that he affirms the innate
openness of humans to receive God's word and the historical
framing of that reception. Since history is not an abstract concept
but refers to concrete cultural experiences and relationships, the
implication of Rahner's theology is that a human person's openness to hear God's word always and everywhere occurs within the
person's concrete cultural experiences.[26] To be theologically precise,

---

Foundations of Christian Faith: An Introduction to the Idea of Christianity,
trans. William V. Dych (New York: Crossroad, 1990), 225–26.

[23] See Miguel H. Díaz, *On Being Human: US Hispanic and Rahnerian Perspectives* (Maryknoll, NY: Orbis Books, 2001), 79–110.

[24] See Duffy who, summarizing Karl Rahner's theological anthropology, argues that "[it] seems axiomatic for Rahner that 'God can only
reveal what man is able to perceive.' The human person is on the lookout for
a *human* word in which God's word may be heard." Stephen J. Duffy, *The
Dynamics of Grace: Perspectives in Theological Anthropology* (Collegeville,
MN: Liturgical Press, 1993), 268–69.

[25] Rahner, *Hearer of the Word*, 138. Emphasis added.

[26] For a theological exploration of culture, see Kathryn Tanner, *Theories of Culture: An Agenda for Theology* (Minneapolis: Fortress Press, 1997).

the word of God that crosses into history always crosses in cultural ways and is always perceived and interpreted culturally. This was the case with the Word of God made flesh in Jesus of Nazareth, and in the life-giving words Jesus shared that have been left for us to interpret in the Bible. Virgilio Elizondo's argument that "the Word of God crossed the border between the eternal and the temporal, between the divine and the human to become Jesus of Nazareth,"[27] suggests and invites this angle of theological interpretation. The legacy of Elizondo's work, especially his reflections on the Galilean and *mestizo* identity of Jesus, leaves little doubt that from the beginning Latinx theologies have been concerned to affirm the particular and "incarnational" nature of the crossing of God's word.[28] When it comes to discerning this crossing, Latinx popular Catholicism offers a distinct and culturally situated privileged source.[29] The texts and religious practices asoci-ated with Latinx popular Catholicism speak to the notion of a compassionate God, a caring God who crosses into human landscapes to accompany marginalized persons in their indi-vidual and communal daily struggles (*las luchas*).[30] They portray

---

[27] See Virgilio Elizondo, "Transformation of Borders: Border Separation or New Identity," in *Theology: Expanding the Borders*, ed. María Pilar Aquino and Roberto S. Goizueta (Mystic, CT: Twenty-Third Publications, 1998), 29. Karl Rahner conveys a similar argument when he maintains that the incarna-tion shows us that God truly arrives at the human condition, enters into and assumes it, and makes the human condition a part of God's very own divine reality. Karl Rahner, *The Trinity* (New York: Crossroad, 1997), 89.

[28] See Virgilio Elizondo, *Galilean Journey: The Mexican-American Promise* (Maryknoll, NY: Orbis Books, 2000).

[29] See Orlando O. Espín, *The Faith of the People: Theological Reflections on Popular Catholicism* (Maryknoll, NY: Orbis Books, 1997).

[30] On la lucha, the struggle, see Ada María Isasi-Díaz, *En la Lucha/ In the Struggle: A Hispanic Women's Liberation Theology* (Minneapolis: Fortress Press, 1993), and Isasi-Díaz, *La Lucha Continues: Mujerista*

a God who crosses to disrupt oppresive relationships, to identify with those most in need, and to mediate life in the midst of
threatening experiences.[31] Among these, the text that conveys a
popular story familiar to many within Latinx communities is the
Nican Mopohua.[32]

Crossings in the *Nican Mopohua*

Nican Mopohua is a Náhuatl expression that translates into
"Here we recount."[33] The expression is the *incipit* of the Guadalupan narrative, and it is also used as the Náhuatl title for the text.[34]
Aptly characterized as "gospel" or good news for the Americas, it is a
culturally situated text that reveals the border-crossing word of God
entering into solidarity with and assuming the face of marginalized

---

Theology (Maryknoll, NY: Orbis Books, 2004).

[31] See Miguel H. Díaz, "On Loving Strangers: Encountering the
Mystery of God in the Face of Migrants," *Word and World* 29 (2009): 239–42.

[32] On issues of origins, authorship, date, and controversies surrounding
the *Nican Mopohua,* see Díaz, *On Being Human,* 69–74.

[33] Elizondo, *Mother of New Creation,* 5.

[34] It is worth noting that there are many traditions and interpretations
related to Guadalupe. Among the most important of these are Sánchez's
Imágen de la Virgen and Luis Laso de la Vega's Náhuatl account titled *Huey
tlamahuiçoltica,* which includes the *Nican Mopohua.* On the significance
of Sánchez's work, which focuses on the connection between Guadalupe
and Revelation 12, and on the significance of de la Vega's work, which
focuses on promoting Guadalupe among Náhua audiences, see Jean-Pierre
Ruiz, "Biblical Interpretation from a US Hispanic American Perspective:
A Reading of the Apocalypse," in *El Cuerpo de Cristo: The Hispanic Presence in the US Catholic Church,* ed. Peter Casarella and Raúl Gómez (New
York: Crossroad, 1998), 90–96. For a study that raises several objections
regarding the authenticity of the Guadalupan narrative, see Stafford Poole,
*Our Lady of Guadalupe: The Origins and Sources of a Mexican National
Symbol, 1531–1797* (Tucson, AZ: University of Arizona Press, 1995).

human persons.[35] Above all, the story of Guadalupe highlights God's power to heal, resurrect, and build inclusive community.

The protagonist of this story is Juan Diego, a sixteenth-century indigenous person, whose life, similar to the lives of other indigenous persons, came under threat as a result of the Spanish conquest. Juan Diego suffers from the effects of social othering and communal disintegration. Similar to Jesus' accompaniment of conquered peoples, Guadalupe walks with a conquered Náhua people. Like Jesus, she speaks life-giving words as the woman who arrives pregnant with God's life.[36] Among other things, the words she speaks concern human agency, healing physical and social illnesses, and the reintegration of persons into inclusive communal relationships. The following selected passages from the story of Guadalupe offer possibilities of interpreting her crossing as a life-giving encounter with Juan Diego and his community.

Restoration and Life-Giving Agency (Nican Mopohua, §12)

One might surmise from the cultural context described in the *Nican Mopohua* that Juan Diego is on the lookout to receive divine revelation. The story begins by telling us that he hears singing from the summit of Tepeyac Hill, a hill associated with the site of the goddess Tonantzin. As he walked this holy ground of his ancestors, the sound of beautiful birds on the summit of the hill catch his attention.[37] The way that this mystical experience is described

---

[35] On the Gospel-like nature of the Guadalupan narrative for the Americas, see Elizondo, *Mother of New Creation*, 103–7.

[36] On the theology of God's arrival in history "pregnant" with life, see Jeanette Rodriguez, "God Is Always Pregnant," in *The Divine Mosaic: Women's Images of the Sacred Other*, ed. Theresa King (Saint Paul, MN: Yes International Publishers, 1994), 112–26.

[37] Elizondo, *Mother of New Creation*, 6–7.

is important for understanding the cultural mediation of the word that crosses. The story uses expressions that meaningfully convey his cultural context (e.g., "when it was still night," "It was already beginning to dawn," *flor y canto*) and frame the revelatory nature of his religious experience.[38] These expressions evoke the familiar and safe space that prepare Juan Diego to receive what he perceives to be divine revelation: "Maybe I am in the land of my ancestors, of the elders, of our grandparents? In the Land of Flower, in the Earth of our flesh? Maybe over there inside of heaven?"[39]

At Tepeyac, Juan Diego encounters Guadalupe, who crosses with words that challenge his oppressive social context and mediate a grace-filled encounter with God. Guadalupe crosses specifically into his cultural context and speaks to him in his Náhuatl tongue, employing religious symbols and expressions common to his people. Above all, she communicates not as foreigner or as a superior being but as one who stands in solidarity with him. She crosses to restore his dignity and empower his human agency: "And when the song finally ceased, when everything was calm, he heard that he was being called from the summit of the hill. He heard: 'Dignified Juan, dignified Juan Diego.'"[40] The life-giving and empowering nature of these words has been amply discussed. Tracing the process of Juan Diego's personal and life-giving transformation, Roberto Goizueta offers the following statement: "The Guadalupan narrative details the moving process through which Juan Diego evolves from being the passive object of other's actions to the active subject of his own future."[41] In this sense, Juan Diego's transformation resonates with biblical narratives of empowerment, such as the healing of the Gerasene.

---

[38] Elizondo, *Mother of New Creation*, 25–78.

[39] Elizondo, *Mother of New Creation*, 7.

[40] Elizondo, *Mother of New Creation*, 7.

[41] Roberto S. Goizueta, "Resurrection at Tepeyac: The Guadalupan Encounter," *Theology Today* 56, no. 3 (1999): 77.

The Healing of Juan Bernardino, Juan Diego's Uncle
(Nican Mopohua, §§60–78)

As the story unfolds, Guadalupe asks Juan Diego to go to the local bishop to petition for the construction of a new church. At first, Juan Diego hesitates to acquiesce to her request. This hesitation is partly attributed to the internalized cultural and oppressive social conditioning that has reduced him to a nobody, a noncredible witness in the eyes of Spanish authorities. But he also hesitates to follow her request out of concern for his uncle who is physically ill and at risk of dying. The tension between death and life and the words Guadalupe speaks in support of physical and social life are articulated in the story of the healing of Juan Diego's uncle.

Some scholars have argued that the illness of the uncle represents more than a physical illness. It symbolizes the cultural trauma brought about as a result of the conquest, especially given the fact that his uncle suffered from smallpox.[42] Regardless of how we interpret the physical and social factors connected to the illness of Juan Diego's uncle, the fact is that Guadalupe utters life-giving words that reassure Juan Diego of his uncle's healing. This physical healing is significant, for it anticipates the social healing of a people, namely, the reincorporation of Juan Diego and his people into an inclusive body of communal relations within the church and society. Just as the Syrophoenician woman in the Gospel of Mark was healed from afar and not in a direct interaction with Jesus, Juan Diego's uncle is also healed from afar and not in a face-to-face encounter with Guadalupe. The life-giving actions of God know no boundaries and borders. As in the Gospel of Mark, faith and trust in the caring God who crosses to heal is enough:

---

[42] Elizondo, *Mother of New Creation*, 73–74.

Listen and hear well in your heart, my most abandoned
son: that which scares you and troubles you is nothing; do
not let your countenance and heart be troubled; do not
fear that sickness or any other sickness of anxiety. Am I
not here, your mother? Are you not under my shadow and
protection? Am I not your source of life? Are you not in
the hollow of my mantle where I cross my arms? Who else
do you need? Let nothing trouble you or cause you sorrow.
Do not worry because of your uncle's sickness. He will not
die of his present sickness. Be assured in your heart that he
is already healed.[43]

These life-giving words that Guadalupe addresses to Juan
Diego are perhaps the most well known and commented-on words
of this story. In Guadalupe, God symbolically and culturally crosses
as a grace-filled presence, arriving as mother and caregiver to those
who have been marginalized and oppressed. Her words suggest
that she adopts Juan Diego as her son. In so doing, she rejects his
sociocultural marginalization and declares him, his uncle, and his
people members of the *familia dei*. Recall how in the stories raised
above in Mark's gospel, Jesus uses healing miracles to reincorporate
marginalized persons into familial and communal relations (e.g.,
the Gerasene, the hemorrhaging woman, Jairus's daughter, and
Syrophoenician woman). By declaring that Juan Diego's uncle has
been healed, Guadalupe interrupts the social plague that threatens
people's lives. By asking for the construction of a new church, she
signals a people's life-giving reconciliation within and reincorporation into community.

---

[43] Elizondo, *Mother of New Creation*, 15–16.

*The Life-Giving Construction of Inclusive Communal Relations
(Nican Mopohua, §§111–12).*

"And when Juan Diego showed where the Lady from Heaven
had indicated that the hermitage should be built, he asked permission to leave. . . . He wanted to go home to see his uncle Juan
Bernardino, the one who had been in his final agony . . . the one
who, the Lady from Heaven had said, had been healed."[44] With these
words, the plot of the story reaches its climax. It is not surprising
that the healing of Juan Diego's uncle already anticipates the fulfillment of Guadalupe's request, namely, the building of the church.
The healing actions of Jesus, as we have seen in Mark's gospel, often
lead to the inclusion, restoration, and communal participation of
marginalized persons. Thus, constructing a new church is less about
building a physical structure than it is about birthing a new way
of being and relating in the world. The story suggests this perspective by telling us that after Juan Diego indicated where to build the
church, he heads to his home to see his uncle, and "they did not let
him go alone; they accompanied him to his home."[45] Guadalupe has
empowered a new way of relating, one that brings about the accompaniment of those that have been marginalized.

In the gospel of Mark, the hemorrhaging woman touches
Jesus' cloak from behind, joining the ranks of so many others who
"begged him that they might touch even the fringe of his cloak"
(Mk 6:56). By touching Jesus, she crosses the boundary of gender
and decorum. The touch leads to new life, it leads to the possibility
of renewing communal relations. In the narrative of the *Nican
Mopohua*, Juan Diego follows Guadalupe's request to fill his cloak
with flowers. When Juan Diego meets the local bishop and opens
his cloak, an image appears in the cloak. The story, which begins

---

[44] Elizondo, *Mother of New Creation*, 21.
[45] Elizondo, *Mother of New Creation*, 21.

with the song of birds, ends with flowers and an image that reflects the humanity of a people. Taken together, *flor y canto,* flower and song, reveal sacred truth for the Náhuatl people.[46] The image of Guadalupe, which results from a "divine touch," denounces the oppressive religious and cultural decorum that have oppressed Juan Diego and his people. It offers an iconic and cultural word that signals their life-giving reincorporation as members of God's family. In this sense, the cloak of Juan Diego becomes a sign that speaks to the healing presence of God amid a broken and sick body that has suffered exclusion as a result of colonial occupation. To summarize: The word of God crosses. It crosses to denounce exclusion. It crosses to build bridges that bring those that have been marginalized from the dehumanizing condition of isolation to the empowering condition of being accompanied.[47]

Ongoing Hope in the Word That Crosses

This chapter carried out a culturally sensitive comparative reading of the Gospel of Mark and the *Nican Mopohua*. It proposed the metaphor of the word that crosses to underscore life-giving encounters in these two texts. The chapter highlighted passages from both the Gospel of Mark and the *Nican Mopohua* as sources that support the notion of a God who crosses borders and boundaries to offer life. The passages I explored suggest that the life of God arrives through persons often associated with the underside of history.[48] They also point to the innate culturally

---

[46] See Roberto S. Goizueta, *Caminemos Con Jesús: Toward a Hispanic/Latino Theology of Accompaniment* (Maryknoll, NY: Orbis Books, 1995), 40.

[47] See Goizueta, *Caminemos Con Jesús*, 47–76.

[48] The expression "the underside of history" is a concept found in Latin American liberation theology and refers to God's saving activity among the poor and marginalized. See, for instance, Linda Martín Alcoff

situated yearning of these persons to hear and encounter the life-giving word of God.

In Christ, God has crossed for the sake of life. Guadalupe as well offers a cultural sign of divine crossing. In solidarity with the Juan Diegos of this world, God continues to struggle against all manifestations of death. This struggle, this *lucha* to affirm life in the form of restoring human agency, healing physical and social illness, and creating inclusive communities can be described as follows:

> The household of God in which we and God dwell together struggles to survive. Forces antithetical to love, communion, and harmony, are active and strong. The final establishment of God's household is an eschatological hope. All of creation groans toward its fulfillment, but the present reality is that of love poised against nonlove and nonbeing. The work of God's reign, the work of all the members of the household, necessarily entails suffering. Mark's gospel clearly perceived the extent to which not only Jesus' life and ministry but also the life of his disciples would cost greatly.[49]

Hope, culturally mediated at Tepeyac, continues to be kept alive as we hear the word of God in the voices of those who undertake multiple crossings for the sake of life in this increasingly globalized and interdependent world. Some of these crossings concern geographical migrations into various countries; some concern internal migrations within countries; still others concern crossing various cultural boundaries. Many of these crossings,

and Eduardo Mendieta, eds., *Thinking from the Underside of History: Enrique Dussel's Philosophy of Liberation* (Lanham, MD: Rowman & Little-field, 2000).

[49] Catherine Mowry LaCugna, *God for Us: The Trinity and Christian Life* (San Francisco, CA: HarperSanFrancisco, 1993), 398.

especially those associated with migrants, immigrants, and exiles, result from what Pope Francis calls the globalization of human indifference.[50] In all of these life-seekers who cross borders and boundaries, we are given the possibility of embracing revelation anew, if we choose to hear the word of God crossing into our landscapes and proclaimed in the words of these neighbors.

---

[50] See Pope Francis, Homily at Lampedusa, July 8, 2013, http:// w2.vatican.va/content/francesco/en/homilies/2013/documents/ papa-francesco_20130708_omelia-lampedusa.html.

2

Beyond Borders and Boundaries

Rethinking Eisegesis and Rereading Ruth 1:16–17

Jean-Pierre Ruiz

The distinguished Cuban American Catholic biblical scholar
Fernando F. Segovia writes, "For cultural studies, all *exegesis* is
ultimately *eisegesis*: interpretation and hermeneutics go hand in
hand."[1] Two decades have passed since these words first appeared
in print, and now Professor Segovia, a past president of the
Academy of Catholic Hispanic Theologians of the United States
(ACHTUS), has also served as president of the Society of Biblical
Literature (SBL), the first SBL president from the Global South.[2]
By no means, however, has this audacious claim of his—that all
exegesis is ultimately *eisegesis*—lost its unsettling edge. I must
confess that there was a time when, as a doctoral student, my

---

[1] Fernando F. Segovia, "Cultural Studies and Contemporary Biblical
Criticism: Ideological Criticism as Mode of Discourse," in *Reading from
this Place*, vol. 2: *Social Location and Biblical Interpretation in Global
Perspective*, ed. Fernando F. Segovia and Mary Ann Tolbert (Minneapolis:
Augsburg Fortress, 1995), 16.

[2] See Segovia's Society of Biblical Literature Presidential Address,
"Criticism in Critical Times: Reflections on Vision and Task," *Journal of
Biblical Literature* 134 (2015): 6–29.

younger and much more naïve self would have pushed back ener-
getically against this dictum, vigorous in the defense of *exegesis*
and in wholehearted agreement with Florence M. Gillman, who
insists that *eisegesis* "is a misguided form of biblical interpretation
that involves reading meaning into a text. In this process an interpreter imposes on the text a meaning alien to it."[3] In this chapter, I
offer a consideration of Latino/a biblical interpretation in light of
the turn to the reader—not the two-dimensional implied reader
that is constructed by reader-response criticism, but to communities of flesh-and-blood readers past and present, *lectores de carne
y hueso*, whose concrete and dynamic reading practices success-
fully subvert the exegesis / eisegesis binary.[4] From the standpoint
of an approach to biblical studies that pushes back against the
false construct of objectivity proposed by the historical critical

---

[3] Florence M. Gillman, "Exegesis / Eisegesis," in *An Introductory
Dictionary of Theology and Religious Studies*, ed. Orlando O. Espín and
James B. Nickoloff (Collegeville, MN: Liturgical Press, 2007), 436.

[4] George Aichele and Gary A. Phillips contend that "the traditional
opposition between exegesis and eisegesis proves unstable," and that "inter-
textuality displaces the reductive binary opposition of exegesis / eisegesis
with 'intergesis,' the term . . . for reading that is the act of rewriting or
inserting texts within some more or less established network. Meaning
does not lie 'inside' texts but rather in the space 'between' texts. Meaning
is not an unchanging ideal essence but rather variable, fluid, and contextual
depending upon the systemic forces at work that bind texts to one another.
On this view meaning can no longer be thought of as an objective relation between text and extratextual reality, but instead it arises from the
subjective, or ideological, juxtaposing of text with text *on behalf of* specific
readers in specific historical / material situations in order to produce new
constellations of texts / readers / readings" (George Aichele and Gary
A. Phillips, "Introduction: Exegesis, Eisegesis, Intergesis," *Semeia* 69–70
[1995]: 14–15). Although their neologism "intergesis" has not made
inroads into the lexicon of academic biblical interpretation (and biblical
studies certainly stands in no need of any more overcomplicated technical
vocabulary), it does offer a healthy corrective to the overly simple either/or
of exegesis vs. eisegesis.

paradigm, this chapter represents an unapologetic embrace of a preferential option for culture. This approach takes the culturally situated perspectives of present-day readers just as seriously as it does the cultural matrices from which the biblical text emerged and within which it has been received in different settings across the centuries. First, I offer an overview of what I identify as three key components of biblical interpretation as practiced *latinamente*. Then, rather than engaging in a purely theoretical discussion, one that would remain so abstract as to be disengaged from the reading strategy I want to foreground, I offer a rereading of Ruth 1:16–17.

Biblical Interpretation Done *Latinamente*

Biblical interpretation done *latinamente* is collaborative, connected, and committed.[5] It is collaborative inasmuch as it challenges the typical academic division of labor between biblical studies and theology, refusing to be boxed in by the mistaken notion that biblical scholarship should restrict itself to excavating what the text once *meant*, leaving the consideration of the text's ongoing significance to constructive theologians. The collaborative quality of biblical interpretation done *latinamente* finds appropriate expression in the phrase *teología de conjunto*, an expression that maps the work of theology not in the first person singular but

---

[5] See Jean-Pierre Ruiz, "The Bible and Latino/a Theology," in *The Wiley Blackwell Companion to Latino/a Theology*, ed. Orlando O. Espín (Malden, MA: Wiley, 2015), 111–27; idem, *Readings from the Edges: The Bible and People on the Move* (Maryknoll, NY: Orbis Books, 2011), especially 13–23, "Good Fences and Good Neighbors? Biblical Scholars and Theologians;" and 34–53, "Latino/a Biblical Studies as Public Theology and the Case of US Immigration Reform." Also see Fernando F. Segovia, "A Theological Reading of Scripture: Critical Problematic and Prophetic Vision in the Aftermath and Crossroads of Disciplinary Transformation," in *Catholic Theological Society of America Proceedings* 65 (2010): 1–18.

in the first person plural in ways that reach beyond the borders of the academy and its insider language to consider the vernaculars in which the biblical text is received by real communities of readers. *Teología de conjunto* was born of necessity, at a time not very long ago when US Latino/a theologians and biblical scholars were so few in number that disciplinary boundaries mattered less than the pressing need to collaborate with each other, to challenge each other and to support each other.[6] What began out of necessity has continued in intentionally interdisciplinary and collaborative initiatives, among them the effort to begin shaping a Latino/a ecumenical theology that bore fruit in *Building Bridges: Doing Justice: Constructing a Latino/a Ecumenical Theology*. In that volume, Latina/o Protestant and Catholic scholars collaborated face-to-face at the 2007 ACHTUS Colloquium and then followed up at a distance to revise first drafts in the light of the collaborative give-and-take. Participants worked together to craft intentionally dialogical and deliberately complementary considerations of power relations and social issues, of the relationship between the Bible and tradition, grace and justification, as well as ecclesiology.[7] Both process and product were collaborative by design, disrupting the linear model of paper presentation followed by response, which is the typical practice at academic conferences, a model that is dialectical at its best and adversarial at its worst.[8]

---

[6] Also see *Teología en Conjunto: A Collaborative Hispanic Protestant Theology*, ed. José David Rodríguez and Loida I. Martell-Otero (Louisville: Westminster John Knox, 1997).

[7] Orlando O. Espín, ed., *Building Bridges: Doing Justice: Constructing a Latino/a Ecumenical Theology* (Maryknoll, NY: Orbis Books, 2009).

[8] In his contribution to *Building Bridges, Doing Justice*, titled "Outside the Survival of Community There Is No Salvation: A US Hispanic Catholic Contribution to Soteriology" (91–111), Miguel H. Díaz demonstrates that the lived daily experience of community has important implications for soteriology.

A second characteristic of biblical interpretation done *latina-mente* is its connectedness. As I have noted elsewhere:

> It takes lived daily experience, *la vida cotidiana* as a primary point of reference. It would be mistaken to suggest that this implies a preferential option for so-called "popular" or "grassroots" biblical interpretation. It does help us to keep in focus the salutary caution that professionally trained biblical scholars in the academy do not hold sole and exclusive access to the biblical text and its significance. It is to this misconstrued job description of "scientific" (meaning academic) exegesis that the Pontifical Biblical Commission applies the woe pronounced in Luke 11:52, "You have taken away the key of knowledge; you did not enter yourselves, and you hindered those who were entering" (NRSV).[9]

---

[9] Ruiz, "The Bible and Latino/a Theology," 116, with a quotation from the Pontifical Biblical Commission, in *The Interpretation of the Bible in the Church* (Vatican City: Libreria Editrice Vaticana, 1993). Gale A. Yee observes that "the negative evaluation of eisegesis is related to two assumptions about the nature of 'correct' exegesis: first, that an objective, value-neutral inquiry into the text is possible in a proper exegesis of the text, and, second, that there is *one meaning*, primarily the author's own, that exegesis wants to discern. The suspicion of the reader of the biblical text is closely allied to the determination of both religious and academic communities to control the interpretation of such a founding text. Interpretation is put into the hands of elites and specialists who are equipped (either by the laying on of hands or with academic degrees) to grasp *the meaning* of the text" (Gale A. Yee, "The Author / Text / Reader and Power: Suggestions for a Critical Framework for Biblical Studies," in *Reading from this Place*, vol. 1: *Social Location and Biblical Interpretation in the United* States, ed. Fernando F. Segovia and Mary Ann Tolbert (Minneapolis: Augsburg Fortress, 1995), 113.

In 2014, Francisco Lozada Jr. and his mentor Fernando F. Segovia published a co-edited volume titled *Latino/a Biblical Hermeneutics: Problematics, Objectives, Strategies*.[10] The list itself of some seventeen contributors serves as testimony that Latino/a biblical interpretation has begun to establish a distinctive footprint in the academy. In September 2015, the *Review of Biblical Literature* published an insightful review of *Latino/a Biblical Hermeneutics* by Tat-siong Benny Liew, also a doctoral student of Segovia's at Vanderbilt. Liew recognizes that the volume invited its contributors—not to mention its readers who are members of the "guild"—to consider three important but too seldom-asked questions: "First, who am I as a biblical scholar? Second, what am I trying to do or accomplish through biblical studies? Third, how do I pursue my biblical scholarship in light of who I am and what I am trying to do?"[11] Liew himself is well-positioned to address these concerns, inasmuch as, together with Fernando F. Segovia and Randall C. Bailey, he co-edited the 2009 Semeia Studies volume, *They Were All Together in One Place? Toward Minority Biblical Criticism*,[12] an important first step in bringing African American, Asian American, and Latina/o biblical interpreters together to consider each other's reading practices and strategies from the standpoint of our own situatedness as members of minoritized communities.

Liew ends his review by posing a vitally important question, one that merits a verbatim citation here:

---

[10] Francisco Lozada Jr. and Fernando F. Segovia, eds., *Latino/a Biblical Hermeneutics: Problematics, Objectives, Strategies*, Semeia Studies 68 (Atlanta: Society of Biblical Literature, 2014).

[11] Tat-Siong Benny Liew, Review of *Latino/a Biblical Hermeneutics: Problematics, Objectives, Strategies*, in *Review of Biblical Literature*, September 9, 2015. https://www.bookreviews.org/pdf/10076_11163.pdf.

[12] Randall C. Bailey, Tat-siong Benny Liew, and Fernando F. Segovia, eds., *They Were All Together in One Place? Toward Minority Biblical Criticism*, Semeia Studies 57 (Atlanta: Society of Biblical Literature, 2009).

As Segovia points out, Latino/a biblical criticism is "a desire for self-assertion and self-introjection"; we can see this on clear display in the beginning of the last contribution to the volume: [Osvaldo] Vena begins his essay by quoting from Mario Benedetti, "Let the whole world know that the South also exists." In other words, Latino/a biblical criticism is at least partly pursued out of a desire for recognition. [Timothy J.] Sandoval puts it even more strongly through a quote of Charles Taylor: "Due recognition is not just a courtesy we owe people. It is a vital human need." What I want to ask is: Whose recognition may Latino biblical criticism be seeking? The concern or anxiety that such work may not make "any sense . . . to [an] audience," "[suffer] from inherent ghettoization," or "be marginalized (further) in the academy" would imply that recognition from the dominant (read: white) biblical studies guild is desired.[13]

This challenging question should not go unanswered: whose recognition is Latino/a biblical criticism seeking? The same is true for such closely related questions as: For whom are Latino/a biblical critics writing, and to whom is Latina/o biblical criticism accountable? On the one hand, early efforts in establishing an academic footprint for Latinas and Latinos in biblical, theological, and religious studies yielded book titles such as *We Are a People: Initiatives in Hispanic American Theology,*[14] and *From the Heart of Our People: Latino/a Explorations in Catholic Systematic Theology.*[15] These represented sincere efforts to claim places at the

---

[13] Liew, Review of *Latino/a Biblical Hermeneutics.*

[14] Roberto S. Goizueta, ed., *We Are a People: Initiatives in Hispanic American Theology* (Minneapolis: Fortress Press, 2001).

[15] Orlando O. Espín and Miguel H. Díaz, eds., *From the Heart of Our People: Latino/a Explorations in Catholic Systematic Theology* (Maryknoll, NY: Orbis Books, 1999).

table for ourselves, selves as understood in the first person plural. They were efforts to resist pressures to assimilate into elitist modes of scholarly production, to reimagine the configurations of centers and peripheries, maps that—more often than not—left us on the wrong side of the borders that someone else had drawn. Nonetheless, the ascent (so to speak) of one of our own—Fernando Segovia—to the presidency of the Society of Biblical Literature should not be taken to mean that Latino/a biblical interpretation has fulfilled its promise or that it has moved from the margins to the center. Nor does the fact that for the first time the 2015 International Meeting of the Society of Biblical Literature was held in Buenos Aires constitute sufficient evidence that the business-as-usual of the academy has been interrupted more than momentarily. In a deeper sense, the questions of recognition and accountability are not resolved within the academy and its credentialing structures and its mechanisms of validation, among them tenure, promotion, and publication in the right venues. The third characteristic of biblical interpretation done *latinamente* takes this to a different level.

Commitment, a third characteristic of biblical interpretation done *latinamente*, recognizes that knowing and doing, interpretation and the effects of interpretation are closely intertwined. Thus biblical scholars working *latinamente* should not seek refuge behind our desks, for, as Pope Francis urged the faculty of theology at the Catholic University of Argentina, we ought to smell of the people and of the road.[16]

Fernando F. Segovia's 2014 SBL Presidential Address, titled "Criticism in Critical Times: Reflections on Vision and Task," is an

---

[16] Letter of His Holiness Pope Francis to the Grand Chancellor of the "Pontificia Universidad Católica Argentina" for the 100th Anniversary of the Founding of the Faculty of Theology," March 3, 2015, https://www.vatican.va/content/francesco/en/letters/2015/documents/papa-francesco_20150303_lettera-universita-cattolica-argentina.html

especially lucid and compelling expression of the committed and engaged quality of biblical scholarship done *latinamente*. It is done *latinamente* not merely because of Segovia's Cuban background and birth, but also because he brings to his scholarship perspectives born in and nourished from the wellsprings of the Global South, identifying himself as "as an outsider-insider in the West, as a child of the Global South, and as an international migrant."[17] Inviting his colleagues in biblical criticism to "imagine an interpretive project for our times," Segovia proposes a critical paradigm that he tentatively designates as "global-systemic," a configuration of the critical task as a matter of bringing "the field to bear upon the major crises of our post–Cold War times."[18] Thus, Segovia argues, "I see no

---

[17] Segovia, "Criticism in Critical Times," 27.

[18] Segovia, "Criticism in Critical Times," 26. Segovia goes on to detail the moves this would involve for biblical scholars in the following terms: "Such conjunction would entail two analytical dimensions. First, it would require interaction with by now well-established discourses regarding each crisis. Second, it would demand interchange with discourses addressing the convergence of crises, the global state of affairs, by way of world theories from the North and alternative theories from the South. The scope is expansive: the world of production (composition, dissemination, interchange) as well as the world of consumption (reception, circulation, discussion). It would thus encompass the following foci of attention: (1) the texts and contexts of antiquity; (2) the interpretation of these texts and contexts, and the contexts of such interpretations, in the various traditions of reading the Bible, with a focus on modernity and postmodernity; and (3) the interpreters behind such interpretations, and their corresponding contexts. The lens is wide-angled: interaction with the other grand models of interpretation is imperative, determined at any one time by the specific focus of the inquiry in question, since all such angles of inquiry are applicable—in one way or another, to one degree or another—to the analysis of the individual crises as well as the global crisis. In effect, just as historical, literary, sociocultural, ideological, cultural, and religious dimensions crisscross the global-systemic, so does the global-systemic impact upon and intersect with all such dimensions" ("Criticism in Critical Times," 26). All this calls for a collaborative posture on the part of biblical scholars, who will

reason why, in the face of our own contemporary times, we biblical critics should not aim for a . . . conjunction of the scholarly and the political."[19] Segovia concludes his call for committed and engaged biblical scholarship with particular eloquence, reaching back nearly a century to recall the 1918 SBL Presidential Address of James Montgomery, who argued that "critics should see themselves first as 'citizens of the human polity' and answer the call of the world." To this, Segovia adds, "Today . . . I, a voice from the Global South, would reiterate that call. I find no better way to do so than by invoking [Pablo] Neruda. If I may be allowed to paraphrase the great Neruda: We have all made a pact of love with criticism; let us now make a pact of blood with the world."[20]

Segovia is well aware that there is more to the dimension of commitment than a grand gesture of love and kinship with the world per se. Commitment begins with a foothold in the particular, and Segovia explains this by adopting the Johannine model of birth and rebirth (taking his cue from John 3). He writes, "To be sure, I was 'born' a Latino critic, insofar as I was a member of such a constituted minority racial-ethnic grouping. At the same time, I was 'reborn' a Latino critic upon consciously appropriating the community ties, marginalized status and minoritarian agenda associated with such a designation."[21] By no means does this particularity imply that engaging in biblical interpretation *latinamente* implies a narrowly construed identity politics of interpretation. To be sure, one need not be Latina/o in order to engage in reading practices that are collaborative, connected, and committed, for these are

---

need to engage the work of specialists in a variety of disciplines in order to effectively assess the global state of affairs.

[19] Segovia, "Criticism in Critical Times," 29.

[20] Segovia, "Criticism in Critical Times," 29.

[21] Fernando F. Segovia, "Toward Latino/a American Biblical Criticism: Latin(o/a)ness as Problematic," in *They Were All Together in One Place*, 200–201.

descriptive characteristics rather than genetic markers of a herme-neutical sort. Yet connectedness and commitment are concrete and specific, not vague and disembodied, for all three wrestle in an arena where identities are complex constructions of what is given versus what is claimed, what is accepted versus what is resisted.[22]

Reading Ruth 1:16–17 *Latinamente*

With all that in mind, we can turn to consider Ruth 1:16–17.

> Ruth replied, "Do not urge me to leave you, to turn back and not follow you. For wherever you go, I will go; wherever you lodge, I will lodge; your people shall be my people, and your god my god. Wherever you die, I will die, and there I will be buried. Thus and more may the LORD do to me if anything but death parts me from you." (*Jewish Publication Society* version)

How might these words resonate in the ears of a woman who has made her way through the Sonoran desert from Mexico across the southern border of the United States into Arizona? What might this woman have to say to her *comadre* Ruth, who has chosen to leave Moab behind and to bind herself by oath to Naomi, to Naomi's people and Naomi's god? What advice might they exchange with each other about survival strategies for life in lands not their own? What words might be exchanged in a conversation she might have with Orpah, who chose to remain in her own homeland as her mother-in-law returned to Beth-lehem? For that matter, what might she have to say to Naomi, who returned to her own homeland after an absence of many years? Attending to questions like these would be well out of

---

[22] See Ruiz, "The Bible and Latino/a Theology," 118–19.

bounds for a strictly *exegetical* consideration of the biblical text. I would also argue that there is something more than *actualiza-tion* at work here if actualization is to be understood simply as a matter of applying the message of the biblical texts "to contem-porary circumstances and to express it in language adapted to the present time."[23] I would suggest that such conversations might be approached through what Athalya Brenner has called a bidi-rectional reading of the book of Ruth, a reading in which ancient and contemporary narratives and their ancient and contempo-rary contexts shed light on and interrogate each other.[24] I would

---

[23] Pontifical Biblical Commission, *The Interpretation of the Bible in the Church* (Vatican City: Libreria Editrice Vaticana, 1993). The Biblical Commission rightly cautions that *actualization* "cannot mean manipula-tion of the text. It is not a matter of projecting novel opinions or ideologies upon the biblical writings, but of sincerely seeking to discover what the text has to say at the present time. The text of the Bible has authority over the Christian church at all times, and, although centuries have passed since the time of its composition, the text retains its role of privileged guide not open to manipulation."

[24] Athalya Brenner, "From Ruth to the 'Global Woman:' Social and Legal Aspects," *Interpretation* 64, no. 2 (April 2010): 162–68. Brenner juxtaposes the situation of Ruth with the predicament of migrant workers who are foreign nationals (mainly from Thailand and the Philippines) in twenty-first-century Israel. The book of Ruth has inspired a broad range of bidirectional readings. These include Noveen Rao, "The Book of Ruth as a Clandestine Scripture to Sabotage Persian Colonial Agenda: A Paradigm for a Liberative Dalit Scripture," *Bangalore Theological Forum* 41 (2009): 114–34; Julie Li-Chuan Chu, "Returning Home: The Inspiration of the Role Dedifferentiation in the Book of Ruth for Taiwanese Women," *Semeia* 78 (1997): 47–53; Musa W. Dube, "The Unpublished Letters of Orpah to Ruth," in *A Feminist Companion to Ruth and Esther*, ed. Athalya Brenner (Sheffield, Eng.: Sheffield Academic Press, 1999), 145–50; Laura E. Donaldson, "The Sign of Orpah: Reading Ruth through Native Eyes," in *A Feminist Companion to Ruth and Esther*, 130–44; Gale A. Yee, "'She Stood in Tears amid the Alien Corn': Ruth, the Perpetual Foreigner and Model Minority," in *They Were All Together in One Place*, 119–40; Mercedes Lopes, "Alianza por la vida: Una lectura de Rut a partir de las culturas,"

also suggest that this approach sidesteps the temptation to engage in a simply correlational reading, whereby—as Francisco Lozada explains—the biblical text "is seen as a mirror of sorts between the world behind the text and the world in front of the text (reader). Thus the text is an avenue that joins the current Latino/a experience and reality within the biblical text."[25] Lozada correctly characterizes the hermeneutical approach taken in *Readings from the Edges* as one that avoids a consideration of the biblical text via correlation and that likewise steers clear of considering the biblical text only as a dialogue partner. Rather, he suggests that my approach treats the biblical text as ideological, explaining, "This particular tactic involves the employment of the text as a point of departure to explore issues related to Latino/a identity. In other words, it is not just the text that undergoes explorative analysis of its composition but also aspects of the reader and her or his community."[26]

Ruth's words in 1:16–17 take up the language of Naomi's exhortation in 1:15, "See, your sister-in-law has returned to her people and her gods. Go follow your sister-in-law." "Do not press me to leave you to turn back from following you," Ruth insists. Tamara Cohn Eskenazi and Tikva Frymer-Kensky observe that

---

Revista Bíblica Latinoamericana 26, no. 1 (1997): 96–101; María Antonia Marques, "Los caminos de sobrevivencia: Una lectura del libro de Rut," *Revista Bíblica Latinoamericana* 63, no. 2 (2009): 66–73. US Latino/a readings include Francisco García-Treto, "Mixed Messages: Encountering *Mestizaje* in the Old Testament," *Princeton Seminary Bulletin* 22 (2001): 150–71; Robert Maldonado, "Reading *Malinche* Reading Ruth: Toward a Hermeneutic of Betrayal," *Semeia* 72 (1997): 91–109. Also see Judith A. Kates and Gail Twersky Reimer, *Reading Ruth: Contemporary Women Reclaim a Sacred Story* (New York: Ballantine Books, 1994).

[25] Francisco Lozada Jr., "Toward Latino/a Biblical Studies: Foregrounding Identities and Transforming Communities" in *Latino/a Biblical Hermeneutics*, 196.

[26] Lozada, "Toward Latino/a Biblical Studies," 197–98.

"the verb 'leave' in English focuses on the one who is departing whereas Ruth's language focuses on the one who will be abandoned and whom she refuses to abandon. The term carries theological weight when God promises not to forsake Israel (Deut 31:6, 8) or when used for apostasy (Josh 24:20)."[27]

"Your people shall be my people, and your god my god," Ruth assures her mother-in-law, a pledge she seals with an oath sworn in the name of Naomi's god.[28] Despite this solemn promise, Ruth continues to identify herself as a foreigner (2:10). Once she arrives in Naomi's homeland, she is regularly identified as "Ruth *the Moabite*" (1:22; 2:2; 4:10), with her Moabite origin specified *twice* by Boaz's servant in response to his master's question about whose property Ruth is ("Whose girl is that?" [2:6]). The question itself is unsettling, for with it Ruth is reduced to being someone else's property. The servant's response, "She is a *Moabite* girl who came back with Naomi from the country of *Moab*," does not quite answer the question, but it very emphatically underscores Ruth's foreignness, erasing her own proper name and associating her with Naomi.

In a narrative in which dialogue is such a prominent feature (direct speech is found in fifty of the book's eighty-five verses), it is noteworthy that on two occasions (2:2 and 2:21) it is the narrator who introduces direct speech addressed by Ruth to Naomi with "Ruth *the Moabite* said," marking her words this way only after she has arrived in Bethlehem.[29] Yet neither the narrator nor any of the characters in the book provide the reader with any clues about what baggage—positive, pejorative, or otherwise—accompanies the frequent designation of

---

[27] Tamara Cohn Eskenazi and Tikva Frymer-Kensky, *The JPS Bible Commentary: Ruth* (Philadelphia: Jewish Publication Society, 2011), 20.

[28] See Mark S. Smith, "'Your People Shall Be My People': Family and Covenant in Ruth 1:16–17," *Catholic Biblical Quarterly* 69 (2007): 242–58.

[29] In her bidirectional reading of Ruth from an Asian American Perspective, Gale A. Yee describes Ruth as a "perpetual foreigner" (Yee, "'She Stood in Tears amid the Alien Corn,'" 130–33).

Ruth as a Moabite. Exegetically speaking, the interpreter of Ruth faces a problem, one that Jeremy Schipper states succinctly: "Why does the book refer to its title character's ethnicity so often?"[30]

The text of the book itself is entirely neutral about Elimelech's decision to make his way to Moab with Naomi and their two sons (1:2), and the book is equally neutral about Mahlon and Chilion taking Moabite wives (1:4).

What is to be made of this in the light of texts like Numbers 25:1–5, in which the LORD's anger was kindled against Israel because at Shittim the people began to have sexual relations with the women of Moab, and 1 Kings 11:1–2, where Solomon violates the divine prohibition against marrying foreign women, including Moabites? What of the status of Moabites as presented in Deuteronomy 23:3–6?

> No Ammonite or Moabite shall be admitted to the assembly of the LORD. Even to the tenth generation, none of their descendants shall be admitted to the assembly of the LORD, because they did not meet you with food and water on your journey out of Egypt, and because they hired against you Balaam son of Beor, from Pethor of Mesopotamia, to curse you. . . . You shall never promote their welfare or their prosperity as long as you live.

What of the prohibition against exogamous marriage found in Ezra 9?[31] While the text of Ruth refrains from passing judgment on the actions of Elimelech and his sons, the same has not been

---

[30] Jeremy Schipper, *Ruth: A New Translation with Introduction and Commentary*, Anchor Yale Bible, vol. 7d (New Haven, CT: Yale University Press, 2016), 40.

[31] See Cheryl B. Anderson, "Reflections in an Interethnic / Racial Era on Interethnic / Racial Marriage in Ezra," in *They Were All Together in One Place*, 47–64.

true for many of the book's readers. With respect to the deaths of Elimelech's two sons, simply reported without any explanation in the Hebrew text, the Targum concludes that this was due punishment for their sin of marriage with Moabite women:

> They transgressed against the decree of the Memra of the Lord and they took for themselves *foreign* wives *from the daughters of Moab*. The name of one was Orpah and the name of the second was Ruth, *the daughter of Eglon, king of Moab*, and they dwelt there for about ten years. *And because they transgressed against the decree of the Memra of the Lord and intermarried with foreign peoples, their days were cut short* and both Mahlon and Chilion also died *in the unclean land*, and the woman was *bereaved* of her two sons and *widowed* of her husband. (Ruth R. 1:4–5)[32]

Still other ancient interpreters attribute their fate to the misdeed of leaving Bethlehem for Moab.[33]

Schipper appropriately asks, "As Ruth never addresses attitudes reflected in the texts that seem to disparage Moabites, one may ask whether Ruth's failure to assess Moabites negatively is best explained as a polemic against negative attitudes that are never referred to or addressed in the text."[34] The book's complete silence

---

[32] The italicized text represents material added in the Targum. The translation is from Kevin Cathcart, Michael Maher, and Martin McNamara, eds., *The Aramaic Bible: The Targum of Ruth and Chronicles*, Aramaic Bible 19 (Collegeville, MN: Liturgical Press, 1994). The translation of the Targum of Ruth in this edition is by D. R. G. Beattie.

[33] See Danna Nolan Fewell and David Miller Gunn, *Compromising Redemption: Relating Characters in the Book of Ruth* (Louisville: Westminster John Knox, 1990), 121; Cynthia Ozick, "Ruth," in *A Feminist Companion to Ruth*, 197–99; Leila Leah Bronner, "A Thematic Approach to Ruth in Rabbinic Literature," in *A Feminist Companion to Ruth*, 146–69.

[34] Schipper, *Ruth*, 38.

vis-à-vis what value—negative or positive—is to be assigned to the persistent designation of Ruth as a Moabite is exegetically unsettling inasmuch as the book itself offers no clues as to whether or not it should be considered, in Schipper's terms, as "as a polemic against condemnations of exogamy or against negative stereotypes of Moabites."[35]

At the very least, the persistent identification of the book's protagonist as a Moabite marks her as a foreigner, an outsider, someone who does not completely belong among those with whom she finds herself in Bethlehem. How might such othering of the perpetual foreigner from beyond the borders of the book resonate in the ears of Ruth's twenty-first-century border-crossing *comadre*? What advice might she have to offer her *comadre* Ruth about getting by in a land that will never really be her own, on the basis of her own experience of life in a land where some will always label her "illegal" because she crossed the border with many needs but without the appropriate papers? Oath or no oath, she would likely tell Ruth that in Bethlehem she will *always* be othered as the Moabite who came from Moab, however fluent she might become in the language and the culture of her adopted land.

What of the second part of Ruth's promise to Naomi? Paralleling her declaration, "Your people will be my people," she likewise swears, "Your god will be my god." While the henotheistic connection between a people and their god in the narrative world of the

---

[35] Schipper, *Ruth*, 40. Schipper proposes that Moabites are to be understood as descendants of Lot, the son of Abram's brother Haran (Gn 11:27). Thus, "As a foreigner-kinswoman, the title character epitomizes the Moabite in the book of Ruth as not simply a foreigner but kin who has become foreign through ten generations of separation since the time of Isaac and Lot" (*Ruth*, 41, 44). As intriguing as Schipper's suggestion may be, it falls short of resolving the tension between the frequent identification of its protagonist as a Moabite and the book's silence vis-à-vis positive or negative connotations of that designation. In effect, the decision is left to interpreters beyond the borders of the text.

text is not troublesome in terms of the different choices made by
Orpah on the one hand and Ruth on the other, Ruth's "conversion"
from her Moabite gods to Naomi's god is cause for considerable
attention in traditional Jewish interpretation. There the story is
reread (and even rewritten) to characterize Ruth as a righteous
proselyte. As Leila Leah Bronner writes, "The sages [find] themselves needing to 'justify' her affiliation with the Jewish people,
hence they seek to make her conversion 'kosher' by rationalizing
it halakhically."[36] Consider, for example, what the Targum adds to
Ruth 1:16–17, highlighted here in italics:

> Ruth said, "Do not urge me to leave you, to go back from
> after you for *I desire to be a proselyte." Naomi said, "We are
> commanded to keep Sabbaths and holy days so as not to walk
> beyond two thousand cubits." Ruth said, "Wherever you will
> go, I will go."* Naomi said, *"We are commanded not to lodge
> together with gentiles."* Ruth said, "Wherever you lodge, I
> will lodge." *Naomi said, "We are commanded to keep six
> hundred and thirteen precepts." Ruth said, "What your
> people keep I will keep as though they were my people from
> before this." Naomi said, "We are commanded not to engage
> in idolatry."* Ruth said, "Your god is my god." *Naomi said,
> "We have four death penalties for the guilty, stoning with
> stones, burning with fire, execution by the sword and cruci-
> fixion." Ruth said,* "By whatever means you die, I will die."
> *Naomi said, "We have a cemetery." Ruth said,* "And there I
> will be buried. *And do not say any more.* May the Lord do
> thus to me and more *to me,* if even death should separate
> me and you." (Targum of Ruth 1:16–17)

---

[36] Bronner, "A Thematic Approach to Ruth in Rabbinic Literature,"
148, and also see 148–153.

The Targum has Ruth explicitly voice the desire to become a proselyte, and where the Hebrew text of Ruth 1:16–17 is a continuous and uninterrupted response to Naomi's urging that she return to Moab, the Targum refashions this material as a dialogue between Ruth and Naomi, in which each phrase pronounced by Ruth is an appropriate response to Naomi's explanation of what becoming a proselyte would involve.[37] Thus, in the Targum 1:18 becomes not only Naomi's perhaps reluctant acquiescence to Ruth's decision, but an indication of Naomi's confidence in the sincerity of Ruth's desire to become a proselyte: "When Naomi saw that she was determined to go with her, she said no more to her" (*NRSV*).

Cohn Eskenazi and Frymer-Kensky tell us that in 1:16–17, Ruth finds herself at a crossroads. They also point out that "whatever transformation takes place at this moment, it is not perceived within the narrative as an altered ethnic or communal identity." They ask, "Would the text's original audience have understood that Ruth could unilaterally declare herself to be part of Naomi's people?"[38] Neil Glover correctly maintains that it is not by her own saying so that Ruth becomes part of Naomi's people. In the book of Ruth, identity is a matter of the first person plural. Glover identifies three specific moments in the text where the recognition of Ruth's new allegiance and new identity find expression inasmuch as her name appears without the Moabite tag. The first is 2:8, where Boaz addresses her not by name but as "my daughter." The next is in 2:22, where the narrator introduces Naomi's words with "Naomi said to Ruth, her daughter-in-law," and where Naomi addresses Ruth as "my daughter."

---

[37] On rabbinic views of intermarriage and conversion in response to Ruth, see Cohn Eskenazi and Frymer-Kensky, *The JPS Bible Commentary: Ruth*, xlv–xlvi.

[38] See Cohn Eskenazi and Frymer-Kensky, *The JPS Bible Commentary: Ruth*, 21–22.

The question of *religious* conversion would not be foreign to
Ruth's twenty-first-century immigrant *comadre* interlocutor, and
the issue of shifts in affiliation by Latin American immigrants to
the United States from Catholicism to evangelical Protestantism
and Pentecostalism has caused no small amount of consterna-
tion among the leadership of the Roman Catholic Church in the
United States. As early as 1988, Andrew Greeley sounded an alarm
about "defection" among Hispanics, calling this "an ecclesiastical
failure of unprecedented proportions."[39] While shifting trends in
religious affiliation should surely be the object of careful attention
on the part of social scientists and theologians, along with well-
informed pastoral planning by church leaders, the alarmist rhetoric
of "defection" can only be counterproductive.

Consider, for example, Michael Paulson's May 8, 2014, *New
York Times* article titled "Even as US Hispanics Lift Catholicism,
Many Are Leaving the Church Behind."[40] Paulson cites statistics
from the Pew Research Center's May 7, 2014, report, "The Shifting
Religious Identity of Latinos in the United States," according to
which in 2013, 55 percent of Hispanics in the United States identified themselves as Catholic, a decrease from 67 percent in 2010,
and according to which "about 22 percent of Hispanics identify as
Protestant—including 16 percent who say that they are evangelical
or born-again—and 18 percent say they are unaffiliated."[41] Paulson

---

[39] Andrew M. Greeley, "Defection among Hispanics," *America* 159
(July 30, 1988): 62. See Paul Perl, Jennifer Z. Greely, and Mark M. Gray,
"What Proportion of Adult Hispanics Are Catholic? A Review of Survey
Data and Methodology," *Journal for the Scientific Study of Religion* 45, no. 3
(September 2006): 419–36.

[40] Michael Paulson, "Even as US Hispanics Lift Catholicism, Many
Are Leaving the Church Behind," *New York Times*, May 8, 2014, https://
www.nytimes.com/2014/05/08/upshot/even-as-hispanics-lift-catholicism-
theyre-leaving-it.html

[41] Paulson, "Even as US Hispanics Lift Catholicism, Many Are

quotes Pew senior researcher Cary Funk, who notes, "It's surprising partly because of the size of the decline in a short period," and who also observes, "We're also seeing an increase in religious pluralism among Hispanics and also greater polarization along the religious spectrum."[42] Then Paulson goes on to cite a July 5, 2014, *Huffpost Religion* blog post by Sister Mary Ann Walsh, who at that time was serving as director of media relations for the United States Conference of Catholic Bishops. Commenting on "the reality that the United States has become a secular society," Walsh goes on to warn:

> Everyone, including Hispanics, and especially young ones, can fall prey to what has become a new American problem, religious relativism, where, perhaps inspired by exciting music or a rousing preacher, you move from your parents' church to another to no church at all. That's the climate in which we are forming our youth, the future of the Catholic Church and US society. It is scary to consider that religious relativism may be the greatest threat that exists to the increasingly important Hispanic Catholic community.[43]

Whatever else may be said about the Pew report's statistics, the numbers themselves do not speak either simply or unambiguously about a phenomenon that is ultimately about people's decision-making regarding the commitments involved in religious

---

Leaving the Church Behind," 20. He cites statistics from Pew Research Center, May 7, 2014, "The Shifting Religious Identity of Latinos in the United States," https://www.pewresearch.org/religion/2014/05/07/the-shifting-religious-identity-of-latinos-in-the-united-states/

[42] Paulson, "Even as US Hispanics Lift Catholicism, Many Are Leaving the Church Behind," 21.

[43] Mary Ann Walsh, "Good News: Many Hispanic Catholics. Challenge: To Meet Their Spiritual Needs," *Huffpost Religion*, May 5, 2014. https://www.huffpost.com/entry/good-news-many-hispanic-c_b_5267339.

belonging. Walsh's posting was an expression of her own opinion and not by any means an official statement by the United States Conference of Catholic Bishops. Yet her panicked claim that Hispanics are in danger of falling prey to religious relativism, with young people "perhaps inspired by exciting music or a rousing preacher" moving away from their parents' religious affiliation "to another [church] to no church at all" seems inappropriate for someone who served as media relations director for a bishops' conference that has since proudly marked the fiftieth anniversary of *Dignitatis Humanae*, the Second Vatican Council's Declaration on Religious Freedom.

Here Ruth might speak across the centuries to her immigrant *comadre* from Latin America and perhaps even offer a word or two to her *comadre's* bishops and their staff to explain that religious switching is not *only* about religion, strictly speaking. Ruth's decision to embrace Naomi's people and Naomi's god has far less to do with the particulars of religious practice at Bethlehem in Judah than it had to do with connecting and belonging, with the relationship with her mother-in-law to which Ruth commits herself. It is, in effect, a preferential option on Ruth's part to participate in her mother-in-law's culture. Ruth's decision to embrace her mother-in-law, her mother-in-law's people, and her mother-in-law's god is solemn and deliberate, sealed by an oath. Equally free to decide her own future and to determine her own allegiances, her sister-in-law Orpah decides otherwise. She kisses Naomi good-bye and then returns to her land and to her gods, and the text says not a single word to suggest that hers is the wrong decision.[44] When it comes to the twenty-first-century *comadres* of Ruth and

---

[44] Cohn Eskenazi and Frymer-Kensky point out that "later Rabbinic midrashim evaluate Orpah's action differently. They describe violent consequences as a result of her departure from Naomi: after leaving, she is repeatedly brutalized and raped" (*JPS Bible Commentary: Ruth*, 17).

Orpah in the world in front of the text, would it not be more prudent to respect the decisions they make vis-à-vis religious, national, and cultural affiliations, and to understand the reasons for which they choose as they do?

Biblical Interpretation as Collaborative, Connected, and Committed

Much more could be said about the conversation across the centuries and across the text between Ruth and her twenty-first-century immigrant and refugee *comadres*. By way of conclusion, I want to suggest that this way of framing a multilateral and diachronic conversation between the rich and complex world of the book of Ruth and the no less rich and by no means any less complex world in front of the text in our own time offers a fruitful entrée into the way I have characterized Latino/a biblical interpretation as collaborative, connected, and committed. Why bother reading Ruth? Engaged reading, intimately bound up with the particulars of lived daily experience in communities past and present, enters into conversation with the biblical text in ways that make a difference not only in the way in which readers understand the significance of the text, but, even more urgently, in how readers shape and share our own responsible living in the world in front of the text. As a contribution to a wider discussion of the preferential option for culture in Latino/a biblical studies and theologies, I hope that the reading of Ruth 1:16–17 I have proposed here makes it abundantly clear that decisions around family, language, religious commitment, and identity have long been—and continue to be—fraught with enormous (and perduring) challenges.

3

A "Preferential Option"

A Challenge to Faith in a Culture of Privilege

María Teresa Dávila

The "preferential option," one of the central and most important insights in Christian theology in the twentieth century, falters upon its arrival on US shores.[1] In the context of privilege, "the preferential option for"—the poor, history, the marginalized, youth, culture—goes head to head with the preferential option *for the culture wars* in the United States. As an *option for* culture, it is a decentering concept that embodies God's love becoming incarnate in our own suffering, poverty, and contexts.

In its emphasis on the church of the poor, Vatican II laid the foundation for what would become "the preferential option for the poor."[2] Latin American bishops and theologians returned from the

---

[1] See, for example, Carmen Marie Nanko, "Justice Crosses the Border: The Preferential Option for the Poor in the United States," in *A Reader in Latina Feminist Theology: Religion and Justice*, ed. María Pilar Aquino, Daisy L. Machado, and Jeanette Rodríguez (Austin, TX: University of Texas Press, 2002), 177–203.

[2] Paul VI, *Constitution of the Church in the Modern World* (*Gaudium et Spes*) (December 1965), §1, http://www.vatican.va/archive/hist_councils/ii_vatican_council/documents/vat-ii_const_19651207_gaudium-et-spes_en.html.

council with the charge to be church in those places where suffering people clamored for a witness of solidarity, spiritual poverty, and prophetic denunciation of injustice and oppression, along with proclamations of liberation in history. The phrase "the preferential option for the poor" is both the culmination and ongoing challenge of Vatican II. It encompasses the theological drive of a church that seeks to reach beyond itself to proclaim integral liberation and mercy to the human family.

And yet in the US context this remains a challenge, articulated in certain pockets of Catholic life, but effectively interrupted in its ability to truly shape the ethos of the church in the United States. Too long beholden to the paradigm of the human person as an individual with a basket of rights and duties protected constitutionally, the Catholic Church in the United States is hard-pressed to present a proper Christian anthropology of the person in community, with full dignity before God and others, but also intimately interdependent in the human web of responsibility and care for others and for creation. As a result, the demands of Catholic social thought, and more specifically of "the option for," seem at best the particular call for a saintly few, at worst the Marxist infection of the cultural revolution of the 1960s in which Vatican II takes place and liberation theology develops. Amid a political and economic culture grounded in utilitarian capitalist individualism, militarism, and racism,[3] a theological and ethical option grounded in the self *for others* and the witness of the servant leadership of Christ seem not only foolish but also radically antipatriotic.

I first began to explore the preferential option for the poor in the US context specifically because of this stark realization.

---

[3] Martin Luther King Jr., "The Three Evils of Society," address delivered at the National Conference on New Politics, August 31, 1967. Transcript available at https://www.scribd.com/doc/134362247/Martin-Luther-King-Jr-The-Three-Evils-of-Society-1967.

During the early spring of 2003, as the administration of then-US President George W. Bush was drumming up support for a preemptive war against Iraq, most Christian leaders in the United States, including bishops from Bush's own denomination, the United Methodist Church, the US Catholic bishops, as well as Pope John Paul II, warned that there was no legitimate ethical rationale for preemptively going to war.[4] And yet at the ground level, in parishes, newspapers, and other venues of Catholic public expression, support for the war was predominant. Perhaps in an effort to support parish families with men and women in the military, preaching too often aligned with President Bush's proposed rationale of going to war for the freedom of the Iraqi people and the safety of the American people than with John Paul II's plea to prevent the reckless slaughter of many. Culturally, many US Catholics were unable to escape the militarist ideology that, along with unbridled capitalism and racism, weaves through our churches. The stark dissonance between the Christian call for a decentering option for others and the reality of the US churches signals that embracing this insight will take nothing short of a cultural revolution.

The development of the *preferential option for culture* in Latino/a theology remains today one of the most promising concepts in the theological academy, where the challenges of "the preferential option for" meet the realities of *lo cotidiano* within a

---

[4] Compiled by Religious News Service, "Religious Groups Issue Statements on War with Iraq," Pew Research Center, *Religion and Public Life* (March 19, 2003), https://www.pewforum.org/2003/03/19/publicationpage-aspxid616/; John Paul II, "Address to the Diplomatic Corp" (January 13, 2003), http://www.vatican.va/content/john-paul-ii/en/speeches/2003/january/documents/hf_jp-ii_spe_20030113_diplomatic-corps.html; John Paul II, "Angelus" (March 16, 2003) http://www.vatican.va/content/john-paul-ii/en/angelus/2003/documents/hf_jp-ii_ang_20030316.html; Russell Shaw, "John Paul II was right about Iraq," *Catholic Vote* (April 2, 2019) https://catholicvote.org/john-paul-ii-was-right-about-iraq.

church reluctant to fully embrace the task of being and becoming divine love incarnate in the struggles of others. This option was born amid the experiences of cultural, political, and economic exclusion and marginalization of Latin American immigrants and US-born Latinos/as. Rooted in the struggles of everyday life, Latinos/as theologically developed and explored expressions of life in the Spirit and of a liberative hope in Jesus Christ that characterized how our communities endured and survived. What emerged were grassroots Catholic theologies that were markedly different from mainstream US Catholicism.

Key to Latino/a theology is an anthropology of being for others from the perspective of the marginalized. Latino/a theologies arose from the marginalized. They made an option for the people on the margins. They are lived through concrete acts of solidarity and relationship building. This engagement contrasts with several dominant US Christian views toward those on the margins, typically enacted by white citizens expressing their largess through charity and donations for the less fortunate.

The prevalent narrative within the US context presents a challenge to a "preferential option for," and yet it is also the soil in which Latino/a theology might serve as seed, fertilizer, water, and sun for the flower and the fruit of a truly liberative garden. The cultural revolution to break US Christianity from its collusion with an individualist, hypercapitalist, militarist, and racist heritage might just come from the pages and practices of Latino/a theologies and other theologies from the margins. Building a church where *a preferential option for* is a central mark of Christian discipleship will depend on our ability to see the church in the United States as a community of resistance to the impulses that too easily drive us to be nationalist and to support market forces, individualist interests, and militarist and racist political agendas.

Theology as a Cartographic and Epistemic Task

First, let me explain how I understand the content of the phrase *a preferential option for*. As the incarnational principle of divine love,[5] the phrase demands a location or relocation—a cartography for discipleship in a place outside of privilege. In this place of suffering and rejoicing we encounter church. The church mimics Christ's border crossing into our humanity—from that which depends on nothing, to that which is broken and in need of wholeness. This preferential option is an option *for*, essentially bringing the other in her or his fullness into the center of Christian discipleship. To speak of a preferential option demands carto-graphic, epistemic, hermeneutic, and praxiological processes that echo the rubric of "see-judge-act" so central to Catholic social thought in the second half of the twentieth century.[6] This chapter focuses particularly on the first two, the cartographic task of mapping relocation and epistemology. Both require that attention be given to the ways in which contexts of political, economic, and social privilege impede the right development of a church capable of making such a preferential option.

As an incarnational principle, the preferential option is a Jesuitic concept. It describes the return to the Jesus of the gospels encouraged in Vatican II, and specifically the historical Jesus who is God with us in a specific place, in a specific history marked by imperial and military domination, and dynamics of political and cultural conflict.[7] In other words, there is a place, a location—

---

[5] María Teresa Dávila, "The Role of the Social Sciences in Catholic Social Thought: The Incarnational Principle of the Preferential Option for the Poor and Being Able to 'See' in the Rubric 'See, Judge, Act,'" *Journal of Catholic Social Thought* 9, no. 2 (Summer 2012): 232–38.

[6] Dávila, "The Role of the Social Sciences in Catholic Social Thought."

[7] For a discussion on the central elements of returning to the Jesus of history (as opposed to the study of the historical Jesus), see Orlando O.

historical, cultural, geographic, political, and economic—in which we make the preferential option. There is a cartographic responsibility to situate ourselves as church in the places where those who are suffering are present. But this also demands that we ask profound questions about where each of us stands before making that option. What are our locations of privilege? Where are we most vulnerable? Latino/a theologies propose that even within marginalized communities, we all share in some forms of privilege while still being particularly vulnerable in our spaces. In addition, Latino/a theologies propose that we encounter the vulnerabilities of others as if they were our own. These actions affect the well-being of our communities in ways that an individualist anthropology cannot comprehend. Establishing where we stand is a prior task to being able to "see" in the rubric see-judge-act.

The cartographic task not only expects that we understand the place from which we seek to be church, with all of its privileges and vulnerabilities, it also seeks to decenter us from places of privilege, driving us anew to consider the call to spiritual poverty and our radical dependence on God. This decentering moment is both perceptive and physical. As a first move of any *option for* we turn our sights toward the suffering of others, their experiences of exclusion, poverty, oppression, silencing, and violence. But we also try to be attentive to their hopes, their joys, celebrations, and values. This last element is a particular gift that Latino/a theologies bring to the church in the United States: a strong call for truly seeing the ways that God's liberative Spirit is expressed and found in communities on the margins.

A decentering of perception should also go hand in hand with a physical move to be located within a church in the margins. Pope Francis, through his actions, emphasizes that church is just as

---

Espín, *Idol and Grace: On Traditioning and Subversive Hope* (Maryknoll, NY: Orbis Books, 2014).

importantly about what happens outside of the doors of our build-ings. His visit to migrants on the island of Lampedusa and his Holy Thursday foot-washing ceremonies at various detention centers and jails in Rome are emblematic of this cartographic task with its physical decentering turn to relocate on the margins in order to be in the company of those who suffer.

The Challenge of the Culture of Privilege in the United States

Immediately after the 9/11/2001 attacks on the World Trade Center, then-President George W. Bush told the nation that a sure way to beat the terrorists was to go back to business as usual, specifically to "fly to Disney" and "go shopping."[8] This appeal to the resolve of the American people to resist and restore confidence in the "American way of life" was grounded in commercialism. This presidential advice tapped ideological and philosophical commit-ments about and prevalent definitions of what constitutes personal dignity and the "the good life." These notions have developed in this nation over the past sixty years, and the Catholic Church and other churches in the United States have definitely not been immune.[9] If the cartographic task of the *preferential option for*

---

[8] Frank Pellegrini, "The Bush Speech: How to Rally a Nation," *Time*, September 21, 2001, http://content.time.com/time/nation/article/0,8599,175757,00.html.

[9] See, for example, the discussions on consumerism and theology available in Michelle A. González, *Shopping: Christian Explorations of Daily Living* (Minneapolis: Fortress Press, 2010); William T. Cavanaugh, *Being Consumed: Economics and Christian Desire* (Grand Rapids, MI: W. B. Eerdmans, 2008); and earlier discussions on the challenge of the "Amer-ican Way of Life" to Latino/a theology in Roberto Goizueta's *Caminemos con Jesús: Toward a Hispanic/Latino Theology of Accompaniment* (Mary-knoll, NY: Orbis Books, 1995).

demands decentering and relocation—physical, preferably, but just as important are the spiritual and the political—to be with those who suffer, then this key project and challenge of Vatican II falls entirely flat when it reaches the US shores.

Instead, in the psyche and soul of privilege, there is a preferential option for the self, a preferential option for one truth for myself and those who think like me, a preferential option for order, and inevitably a preferential *option for the culture wars*. Elsewhere, I have referred to the culture wars as a particular US phenomenon that exists alongside three other fetishisms: fetishism of violent conquest of the "other"; fetishism of acquisition and dominion over property; and the fetishism of legal "order" that legitimates the acquisitive impulse.[10] The word "fetishism" in its clinical use brings us to the very real sickness of the soul that these ideologies inflict on the heart of the Christian faithful in the United States.

These ideologies primarily infect the soul with visions of the "good life" that are nothing short of diabolical. Although these dynamics of power and privilege are evidenced in other parts of the world, in the United States they gain the force of religious legitimacy because domination and control of others is entangled with images of a New Jerusalem, a City on a Hill, and Manifest Destiny—images that have long been a part of the nation's preconceptions about its purpose in and under God.[11] Where there is privilege, a spirit of domination marks the quest for human fulfillment and communal living. Among other things, this spirit manifests itself in the neocolonial drive to silence the everyday struggles that question the sacred dichotomies of the public square (left/right, pro-choice/pro-life, legal/illegal, among others). In a

---

[10] María Teresa Dávila, "La Opción Preferencial por los Pobres, Francisco y los EEUU: Obstáculos y Avances," in *Filosofía e Independencia Desde América Latina y el Caribe*, ed. Juan Carlos Casas García (Mexico City: Universidad Pontificia de México, 2016), 139–47.

[11] Dávila, "La Opción Preferencial por los Pobres," 142.

culture of privilege, a *preferential option for order* prioritizes notions of what the good life is. Such a culture draws its legitimacy from the law of domination, individual rights, and the perpetuation of the status quo.[12]

The vision of the human being as an individual in full possession of her or his distinct destiny, able to build herself or himself up totally through her or his own effort, clashes with a faith that asks that we take the context of the other as if it were of existential import to our own destiny.[13] In *Evangelii Gaudium* Pope Francis notes that the joy of the Gospel is in encounter with Christ through encounter with others, warning that "the individualism of our postmodern and globalized era favors a lifestyle which weakens the development and stability of personal relationships and distorts family bonds. Pastoral activity needs to bring out more clearly the fact that our relationship with the Father [*sic*] demands and encourages a communion which heals, promotes, and reinforces interpersonal bonds."[14]

In the US context of privilege, the culture wars present cultural, economic, and philosophical challenges to performing the cartographic task, a re-mapping that must be informed by a faith trained to seek encounter and communion with others. The divisive rhetoric on the issues of reproductive health, marriage equality, economic welfare, immigration policies, racial justice, and other areas reflects a sickly impulse to define one's cause violently over against another's dignity. It also fuels domination of the other and acquisition of material goods that are identified closely with

---

[12] Kelly Brown Douglas, *Stand Your Ground: Brown Bodies and the Justice of God* (Maryknoll, NY: Orbis Books, 2015), 108–29; Dávila, "La Opción Preferencial por los Pobres," 140–47.

[13] Francis, *Evangelii Gaudium* (November 24, 2013), §§63, 67, 78, 89, http://www.vatican.va/content/francesco/en/apost_exhortations/documents/papa-francesco_esortazione-ap_20131124_evangelii-gaudium.html.

[14] Francis, *Evangelii Gaudium*, §67.

notions of the good life. While dressed in cheap religious garb easily provided by various factions in the Christian landscape, the culture wars are wholly opposed to the kind of vision of a community of disciples described by Pope Francis. In light of the sickness of the soul reflected in the aforementioned fetishisms and the pastoral call of Francis to form disciples who build wholeness through relationships, the role of the church must become one of resistance, and even revolution, against pathological attitudes.

Climate change and the environmental crisis are particularly poignant and comprehensive examples of the difficulties of living a preferential option in the context of privilege. Ongoing opposition to a critical assessment of the human impact and the human costs of climate change preceded the 2015 release of Pope Francis's environmental document, *Laudato Si'*.[15] Historically, contentious conversations in the United States have typically followed the release of church documents that challenge the hegemony of market capitalism as naturally good for humanity. Such responses occurred immediately after the release of the pastoral letter *Economic Justice for All* (1986)[16] by the US bishops and the release of John Paul II's *Centesimus Annus* (1991).[17] The case of *Laudato Si'* was no exception.[18] Different elements in the public square debated whether

---

[15] Daniel DiLeo, "Preparing for the Storm: Anticipating and Countering the Likely Attacks on Pope Francis and His Environmental Encyclical," *Millennial*, December 16, 2014, https://millennialjournal.com/2014/12/16/preparing-for-the-storm-anticipating-and-countering-the-likely-attacks-on-pope-francis-and-his-environmental-encyclical/

[16] United States Conference of Catholic Bishops, *Economic Justice for All* (1986), http://www.usccb.org/upload/economic_justice_for_all.pdf.

[17] John Paul II, *Centesimus Annus* (1991), https://www.vatican.va/content/john-paul-ii/en/encyclicals/documents/hf_jp-ii_enc_01051991_centesimus-annus.html

[18] Criticism of *Laudato Si'*, from the measured to the bombastic, abound in various conservative policy and religious opinion outlets. See, for example, R. R. Reno, "The Weakness of *Laudato Si'*," *First Things*, July 1, 2015, https://www.firstthings.com/web-exclusives/2015/07/

Pope Francis's understanding of the science of climate change was sound. Others questioned whether anthropogenesis (i.e., human causes of climate change) could be directly attributed. Francis's solutions to the environmental crisis were critiqued, in part, because many of them demanded a shift in personal self-understanding with respect to cycles of consumption and waste, the global economy, and its direct impact on vulnerable populations.[19]

These discussions are marked by the ill-labeled "left/right" dichotomy of being Christian in the United States. Whereas some see an issue such as climate change as a moral challenge, others see the individual and collective transformations urged in *Laudato Si'* as no more than cultural or economic choices based on personal desire and one's evaluation of the good life, bereft of the transcendental dimension that accompanies a moral imperative, as is clearly stated in the document.[20] Deeper issues are at stake. Climate change, its causes and how to address it, connect with dominant notions of the good life, private property, industry, personal freedom, the proper role of government, consumerism, and other elements of US civil religion.[21] Calls for conversion toward an understanding of a shared destiny for humanity regarding environmental concerns and the just action required to achieve that destiny get lost in the

---

the-weakness-of-laudato-si; and Daniel Mahoney, "'Laudato Si' and the Catholic Social Tradition," *National Review*, October 10, 2015, http://www.nationalreview.com/article/425349/laudato-si-and-catholic-social-tradition-daniel-j-mahoney.

[19] See "Chapter 3: The Human Roots of the Ecological Crisis," in Francis, *Laudato Si'* (May 24, 2015), https://www.vatican.va/content/francesco/en/encyclicals/documents/papa-francesco_20150524_enciclica-laudato-si.html

[20] Francis, *Laudato Si'*, chap. 2.

[21] María Teresa Dávila, "The Option for the Poor in *Laudato Si'*: Connecting Care of Creation with Care for the Poor," in *The Theological and Ecological Vision of* Laudato Si': *Everything Is Connected,* ed. Vincent Miller (London: Bloomsbury, 2017).

cacophony of the public square. Contentious conversations make it almost impossible to reach the transforming and crucial first step of changing one's location, a necessary move for sustained theological and ethical reflection. The same occurs with other targets of the culture wars such as immigration, the affordable care act, same-sex marriage, and economic inequality. The cartographic task requires placing oneself squarely among the ones on the margins—among those who suffer daily the affront of this disordered anthropology that characterizes the American dream. This relocation allows us to perform the epistemic task of seeing in *lo cotidiano* the lives of those who dwell outside of privilege and power. Sadly, this seems an impossibility for the majority of US Christians.

The Latino/a Correction

The cartographic and epistemic turns hinge on the ability to break from a neocolonial modality of conquest and domination of the other. In the culture wars the main weapon of domination is the self-fulfilling notion of truth for me and my own that runs roughshod over those who do not see or experience the world in the same way as those living in privilege. Throughout the past four decades Latino/a theology has offered currents and visions that help identify, resist, and interrupt the idolatry of the culture wars, calling out the ways in which these leave real victims in their wake, stultifying and stunting a discipleship that naturally and organically opts for the other.[22] The preferential option for culture

---

[22] See, for example, Miguel H. Díaz, *On Being Human: US Hispanic and Rahnerian Perspectives* (Maryknoll, NY: Orbis Books, 2001); Orlando O. Espín, *Idol and Grace*; Michelle González, *Created in God's Image: An Introduction to Feminist Theological Anthropology* (Maryknoll, NY: Orbis Books, 2007); Ada María Isasi-Díaz, *Mujerista Theology: A Theology for the Twenty-first Century* (Maryknoll, NY: Orbis Books, 1996); Roberto Goizueta, *Caminemos con Jesús*.

in Latino/a theology resists the neo-imperialist drive for domination by locating the self in the historical and transhistorical journey of the human spirit toward freedom, flourishing, encounter, and communion.[23] Three examples show the ways Latino/a theologies attempt to decenter the violence of the dominant anthropological paradigm that keeps US Christians from truly taking on the tasks associated with a *preferential option for*.

Roberto Goizueta and a Theology of Accompaniment

In *Caminemos con Jesús*, Roberto Goizueta subverts the individualistic anthropology that grounds the myth of the American dream by addressing the relational character of the human being through an anthropology of *nosotros* (we).[24] Goizueta points out the irrational nature of the Enlightenment emphasis on the thinking self, who, absent ties with others, can propel himself or herself into his or her own self-realization. This irrationality, he states, leads to the annihilation of the person, in his or her soul as he or she reaches for self-completion through the violent domination of the other (at an individual and a collective level), and physically, as some fall into the psychological malaise of being alone although materially privileged—and, in the extreme case, resort to substance abuse and suicide.[25]

A theology of accompaniment, *acompañamiento*, acknowledges that Jesus' life is marked by the relationships he built, and the people who walked with him throughout his ministry and accompanied him through his death and resurrection. As an example, Goizueta lifts up the Good Friday processions at the

---

[23] Miguel H. Díaz, "On Loving Strangers: Encountering the Mystery of God in the Face of Migrants," *Word and World* 29, no 3 (Summer 2009): 234–42.

[24] Goizueta, *Caminemos con Jesús*, 47–76.

[25] Goizueta, *Caminemos con Jesús*, 167.

San Fernando Cathedral in San Antonio, Texas. The relational anthropology of Jesus, who walks with his friends and his mother through his ministry, who approaches those in the margins and heals them through close contact, touch, or embrace, is portrayed in the accompaniment of the suffering Jesus and the Sorrowful Mary during the Good Friday procession.[26] For Goizueta, this cultural and religious practice of the *via crucis*, fully embedded in the Hispanic Catholicism of the US Southwest, holds onto the flesh-and-blood representations of Mary, Jesus, Mary Magdalene, the apostles, the centurions, and other characters as reflections of the relationality that exists in their communities.

Accompanying Jesus on the way to the cross witnesses to faith in a Christ that is fully relational and who, on being raised from the dead, moves to embrace his friends and family once again as they prepare to go about the task of building the reign of God. The flesh-and-blood Jesus whom we accompany on Good Friday—his body torn from torture and abuse—and who appears in many Latino homes in images and crucifixes, is the flesh and blood of God with us. For Goizueta, "One cannot understand US Hispanic popular Catholicism without understanding its essentially incarnational and, therefore, relational character: Jesus is not simply a spirit 'out there' or even 'in here'; he lives—as do our families and friends."[27]

In the act of portraying the diverse characters of the passion and crucifixion, these mainly Mexican parishioners connect intimately with their roles—centurion, Mary, John, thief—and through them to all who have participated in the story of redemption throughout history. It is a moment, Goizueta affirms, both radically tied to one's uniqueness as a person before God and radically interdependent with everyone for whom Jesus entered history.

---

[26] Goizueta, *Caminemos con Jesús*, 68–69.
[27] Goizueta, *Caminemos con Jesús*, 69.

Goizueta's theology of accompaniment affirms the cartographic task that requires that we become present in the lives of real persons, those who are poor, living in and on the margins.[28] The option for the poor cannot be an option only for some far-off and removed group of persons. Connecting Christian love for the poor begins with actual relationships of friendship with the poor who are near to us, but whom we often refuse to see. In *Caminemos con Jesús*, Goizueta systematically analyzes the elements in Western capitalist societies that promote an irrational individualist and consumerist self-identity that is counter-relational. He presents a concept that privileges relationality and interdependence, as expressed in scripture, and witnessed to within Latino/a communities. Goizueta perceives, in these intentional moves toward others and away from a preoccupation with self, an antidote for the nationalist and capitalist infections that plague society and church.

Ada María Isasi-Díaz and a Latina Theology of Liberation

In *Mujerista Theology*, Ada María Isasi-Díaz recounts a moment of decentering ritual. As an act of protest during the 1985 Third National Hispanic Pastoral Encuentro in Washington, DC, a group of women organized a rosary on the steps of the National Shrine of the Immaculate Conception. They sought to draw attention to the fact that the documentation arising from the Encuentro, which would be used as the basis for the National Pastoral Plan for Hispanic Ministry, contained no denunciation of the church's unwillingness to allow women full participation. Originally thinking they would have only a few dozen women, the rosary on the steps of the National Shrine drew around five hundred participants, forcing Encuentro organizers to suspend morning activities until it was finished. This

---

[28] Goizueta, *Caminemos con Jesús*, 196–97.

simple prayer, so familiar in the daily lives of Latinas, provided greater visibility to their plight for justice and resulted in the inclusion of a modified statement on the role of women in the church.[29]

For Isasi-Díaz, *mujerista* theology, that is, theology done for and by Latina women for their own liberation and that of other oppressed groups, affirms an understanding of the person as being in community and as bound to others in relationships of mutuality. Ethical concepts such as justice and human rights have no value in themselves as possessed by one person. Rather, these are the result of an interplay of people in power entering relationships of mutuality and transformation with people on the margins.[30] From the perspective of a *mujerista* ethic: "Solidarity will not become a reality unless we are totally committed to mutuality. . . . Commitment to mutuality is what makes it possible for the oppressed and their 'friends' to maintain the revolutionary momentum of the struggle for liberation."[31]

In relationship we come to understand more clearly how oppression works in people's lives, specifically in its gendered and racial dynamics. In the example of the rosary on the steps of the National Shrine, Isasi-Díaz notes how many of their concerns about women's dignity in the church had not coalesced until they all came together. In each other's company, they were able to identify, as a shared concern, the full participation of women in the life of the church, something that had not really arisen in the various separate groups to which they belonged. Their mutual encounter, in solidarity, brought to light dimensions of justice that they had not considered before. Together, they were able to better establish links between what justice might look like in their own communities as well as in the greater church.

Isasi-Díaz learned about the ways Latinas work for liberation in their lives and communities by observing and entering into

---

[29] Isasi-Díaz, *Mujerista Theology*, 199–201.

[30] Isasi-Díaz, *Mujerista Theology*, 94–95.

[31] Isasi-Díaz, *Mujerista Theology*, 99.

relationships with diverse groups of Latinas. In these intentional communities, they share their popular religious practices, considered by some in dominant theological and ecclesial circles to be too primitive or domestic to be of theological or spiritual consequence. Like Goizueta, Isasi-Díaz's work notes the contrast between the dominant US culture and the experience of Latinas who, in and through their daily experiences, seek to open up channels for communal and personal liberation. Latinas, too, must undergo the self-examination of anyone burdened with life in a consumerist and individualist society, where measures of success often demand that we alter our cultural values, and in turn our faith life as well, for profit and the market.[32]

Isasi-Díaz warns that Latinas' struggles for justice, *nuestro proyecto histórico* (our historical project), must never require the objectification of other groups, or the struggle for rights and benefits *for us* at the expense of the rights and benefits of others. This *proyecto* requires strategies that critique social and economic systems as these historically have thrived on the free labor and objectification of others' bodies, especially the bodies of Latinas. Under these conditions, in the current capitalist system, getting "a piece of the pie" simply means grabbing our piece from the very powers that serve to oppress others, including others like us.[33] For Isasi-Díaz, an essential step toward the liberation of all requires *a preferential option for* critiquing that which the dominant economy and culture present as "making it."

Orlando Espín and Traditioning a Compassionate God

At the heart of the Christian message is a decentering that takes place in relationship with Jesus and his witness to a God who is compassionate to all and who is actively transforming the

---

[32] Isasi-Díaz, *Mujerista Theology*, 25, 48, 63.
[33] Isasi-Díaz, *Mujerista Theology*, 154.

world.[34] In Orlando Espín's *Idol and Grace*, this revelation of God
as compassionate, without limits, takes place in the concrete person
of Jesus of Nazareth, who wagers his life on God's transforming
compassion within the context of the margins of an empire, among
the disposable people of his time.[35] Espín's focus on traditioning
makes doctrine, liturgy, ecclesial authority, and other elements of
the church secondary to the message of revelation of a compassionate God and the historical embodiment of this truth through
practices that evidence this compassion without exclusion. Where
these elements serve to bring the faithful closer to the transforming effects of this reality, traditioning lies at the service of the
people of God. Where, however, they take the place of the hope
of the faithful in God's transforming compassion for all, without
exclusion, these elements take on an idolatrous character with its
concomitant violence.[36]

Espín's interpretation of traditioning compels those in
power, whether in the church or in society (and at times, historically, these powers have been one and the same), to examine how
they are living into the radical subversive hope of the majority of
Christians who remain on the margins. This majority, through the
ages mostly illiterate, live out that subversive hope on which they
wager their lives that Jesus was right.[37] Radical subversive hope is
witnessed to in acts of compassion without boundaries and limits,
and oftentimes outside the confines of church life, structures, or
liturgy. Espín acknowledges that traditioning has moments that are
graced as well as idolatrous. Compassion, however, "will be real and
credible if it is truthful and solidarious . . . not self-idolatrous or
reinscribing of power asymmetries . . . gauged by the marginalized

---

[34] Espín, *Idol and Grace*, 4–6, 91.

[35] Espín, *Idol and Grace*, 92.

[36] Espín, *Idol and Grace*, 102–07.

[37] Espín, *Idol and Grace*, 20–22, 32, 37, 42.

disposables themselves, in each of their *cotidianos*, as risk-taking 'enduring with' them."[38] Our faithfulness and humanity are found in our building and living relationships of mutuality and solidarity.

Latino/a Theologies and the Cartographic Task

This brief exploration of the work of three Latino/a theologians witnesses to one of the key tasks of this body of work: to expose the violent consequences of the Enlightenment project of autonomous self-completion when elevated to idolatry within privileged contexts. This violence is especially salient to those speaking theologically from marginalized communities in the United States. In this exposition we must acknowledge the roles that race, gender, ethnicity, and tradition have played in the objectification of the other, especially when the other represents cheap or free labor for the market economy. For too long, the majority in the church in the United States have been content to stay within its doors, disregarding the decentering cartographic requirement of discipleship—the move to be with the other in the margins in imitation of Christ.

The examples of Latino/a theology presented here remind us that Christians ought not to spend our energies tracing a line in the sand, as many of the culture and ideological wars require of their adherents. These wars will make demands of us personally and of our communities, demands grounded in exclusion, in direct opposition to the subversive hope in the all-compassionate God that Espín reminds us is at the heart of the Christian message. Commitment to mutuality in the messiness of the *cotidiano* is inherent in the quest of Latinas for liberation for all persons, so Isasi-Díaz tells us.[39] This mutuality entails an intimate relationship

---

[38] Espín, *Idol and Grace*, 130.
[39] Isasi-Díaz, *Mujerista Theology*, 99–100.

with the incarnate Christ and with each other in history and in our particular stories, as Goizueta's theology of *acompañamiento* suggests. The ideological battles of the culture wars and the ways in which the church contributes to its skirmishes are antithetical to building a beloved community grounded on the preferential option for the poor. A poor church for the poor, as Pope Francis proposes,[40] cannot accommodate ideological battles for political or cultural power. It must depend on a *preferential option for* that which most connects us to Jesus of Nazareth, namely, encounter with the marginalized other.

Latino/a theology seeks to transform the idolatry of "my truth only" to a tapestry of truths weaving a divine arc of truth and justice, built in the messy holiness of the everyday. The task of autonomous self-completion is transformed into notions of being and becoming in a human journey of life toward freedom, communion, and *acompañamiento*. It replaces the primacy of the legal or economic orders with "order" understood as the Spirit's journey toward fulfillment of a larger story, a holy and cosmic story. The work of Alex García-Rivera reveals that this is a story in which the dignity of each builds on the dignity of the whole, from the most personal to the cosmic whole.[41]

Latino/a theology enables and empowers the cartographic and epistemic tasks at the heart of the *preferential option for* by interrupting privilege. We enable the birthing of a transformed church by affirming the preferential option for the poor and by resisting

---

[40] Pope Francis, "Audience to Representatives of the Communications Media," March 16, 2013, http://www.vatican.va/content/francesco/en/speeches/2013/march/documents/papa-francesco_20130316_rappresentanti-media.html.

[41] See, for example, Alejandro García-Rivera, *The Garden of God: A Theological Cosmology* (Minneapolis: Fortress Press, 2009); Alex García-Rivera, *St. Martin de Porres: The Little Stories and the Semiotics of Culture* (Maryknoll, NY: Orbis Books, 1995).

the distorting influences of privilege that make an option for the culture wars or an option for death-dealing fetishisms that honor a drive for power rather than communion or an option for ideological polarization and political divisions. In this new church, the "culture wars" are unmasked as the idols of a privileged, comfortable, and selfish understanding of the good life, and therefore violent to the humanity of all. By enabling the cartographic and epistemic tasks of a preferential option—for culture, for history, for the racial and religious other, for the poor, for youth, for migrants, for the unemployed, for women, for creation—Latino/a theology encourages the decentering practices necessary for resisting the neocolonial dominating impulse of privilege. Instead, a sense of shared journey, encounter, and communion is cultivated and enriched, preparing the way for transformative and graced experiences of faith and discipleship.

4

(De)Ciphering Mestizaje

Encrypting Lived Faith

Néstor Medina

How should we speak about the category and condition of *mestizaje* at a time when biological intermixture and miscegenation and cultural exchange and cross-fertilization are taking place in multiple contexts, in various ways, and at different levels? A number of factors make the category of *mestizaje* both promising and dangerous. The present emergence of identities from the Global South reminds us of the complicated historical racialized and cultural contexts of intermixture; many communities are only beginning to think about how to speak about their own conditions of *mestizaje*. The complexity of the situation is heightened by the global migratory crisis. The displacement and relocation of millions of people worldwide ushers in further possibilities of exchange and intermixture as well as threats of greater ethnoracialized and cultural clashes. Entire sectors of the world's population are left in a state of identity "in-between-ness."[1]

---

[1] The emergence of key theoretical frameworks such as postcolonialism and decolonial thinking also provoke an expansion and deepening of the scope of debates around *mestizaje*. Postcolonial theorists are consid-

For Latinas/os, the breadth of emerging Afro-Latina/o voices, and the increasing activism of indigenous and Afro-Latin Americans enrich, challenge, and complexify ideas of *mestizo* identities, while unveiling a new range of intermixture. As we look at these challenges and shifts in the geopolitical arena, we are compelled to—once again—rethink the scope of *mestizaje.* This entails considering its potential to offer new theological insights without abandoning or lessening the value of earlier theological contributions.[2]

The Multivalence of *Mestizaje*

The notion of *mestizaje* is far from being an obsolete term, particularly because of its capacity to name those identities forged in conditions of historical liminality in the midst of ongoing

---

ering issues of the intersection of identities and the role of colonialism and migration in the construction of hybrid identities not easily definable by closed categories. At the same time, decolonial thinkers wrestle with the effect of *border identities* and thinking, which—according to them—have the potential to disrupt the colonial matrix. See Walter Mignolo, *Local Histories / Global Designs: Coloniality, Subaltern Knowledges, and Border Thinking* (Princeton, NJ: Princeton University Press, 2000).

[2] Of note is the scholarship of pioneer Latina/o scholars who developed the concept of *mestizaje* as *locus theologicus*. See, for example, Virgilio Elizondo, *Mestizaje: The Dialectic of Cultural Birth and the Gospel* (San Antonio, TX: Mexican American Cultural Center, 1978); Virgilio Elizondo, "Mestizaje as a Locus of Theological Reflection," in *The Future of Liberation Theology: Essays in Honor of Gustavo Gutiérrez*, ed. Marc H. Ellis and Otto Maduro (Maryknoll, NY: Orbis Books, 1989), 358–74; Ada María Isasi-Díaz, *En la Lucha / In the Struggle: Elaborating a Mujerista Theology* (Minneapolis: Fortress Press, 1993); Roberto S. Goizueta, "US Hispanic Mestizaje and Theological Method," in *Migrants and Refugees*, ed. Dietmar Mieth and Lisa Sowle Cahill (Maryknoll, NY: Orbis Books, 1993), 22–30. See, too, my analysis in Néstor Medina, *Mestizaje: (Re) Mapping Race, Culture, and Faith in Latina/o Catholicism* (Maryknoll, NY: Orbis Books, 2009).

geopolitical changes. *Mestizaje* bears a multiplicity of meanings, and it addresses different concerns, which may sometimes represent opposing points of view. This multivalent character is both a strength and a source of contestation. No use of *mestizaje* is neutral; it cannot be unlinked from its colonizing history and tendencies even when it is deployed to articulate the voices of excluded communities. That said, the deployment of *mestizaje* as a key theological category is very promising in spite of, and maybe because of, its inherent tensions and contradictions. *Mestizaje* allows us to name the reality of intermixture in its variety of expressions that are irreducible to simplistic categories. Although there are many meanings and nuances associated with the term, for the purpose of clarity, in this chapter I define *mestizaje* in the following four ways.

First, *mestizaje* refers to the biological intermixture that took place between indigenous communities and Iberian peoples as a result of the Spanish and Portuguese invasions of the Americas and the subsequent colonial societies that arose at the end of the fifteenth century. In some instances, the indigenous peoples resisted the invading forces, at times taking Spanish women captive as part of the booty of war, which led to what Alberto Salas has called "*mestizaje al revés*" (reverse *mestizaje*).[3] Two crucial points are worth noting related to gender and racial-ethnic identity. Gender concerns permeate the original encounter between native communities and the invading Portuguese and Spanish forces. The androcentric and patriarchal structures of these encounters violently reduced women to objects of the male colonial gaze and desire.[4] We must go beyond male-centered notions—such as

---

[3] Alberto M. Salas, *Crónica florida del mestizaje de las Indias, siglo XVI* (Buenos Aires, Argentina: Editorial Losada, S.A., 1960), 139.

[4] One good example of the intersections of gender, sexuality, and the male colonial gaze can be found in Amerigo Vespucci's characterization of women's "libidinous" tendencies, which he finds morally reprehensible. See Américo Vespucio, "El Nuevo Mundo: Américo Vespucio a Lorenzo Pier

Octavio Paz's analysis of La Malinche—in attempts to untangle *mestizaje*.[5] Substantive analyses of the role of women in the emergence of *mestizaje* and the perpetuation of the "whiteness" of elite groups are scarce yet necessary.[6] Insufficient attention has been given to race and ethnicity. The African ethnoracial and cultural presence in Latina/o and Latin American contexts deserves its own treatment. The connection, however, with questions of *mestizaje* cannot be underestimated. We must be careful to reclaim the African presences in our Latina/o communities on their own terms and not to obscure their complex identities under the imposed category of *mestizaje*. Some Latinas/os and Latin American scholars subsume the African presences under the notion of *mestizaje*, eclipsing discourses on *mulatez*.[7] The categorizing of the

---

Francesco de Medici," in *El Nuevo Mundo: Viajes y documentos completos*, trans. Ana María R. de Aznar, notes by Fernández Navarrete et al. (Madrid: Ediciones Akal, S.A., 1985), 62.

  [5] Octavio Paz, "The Labyrinth of Solitude," trans. Lysander Kemp, in *The Labyrinth of Solitude and Other Writings* (New York: Grove Press, 1985), 7–212.

  [6] Studies on this topic include Suzanne Bost, "Transgressing Borders: Puerto Rican and Latina *Mestizaje*," *MELUS* 25, no. 2 (Summer 2000): 187–211; Susan Kellogg, "Depicting Mestizaje: Gendered Images of Ethnorace in Colonial Mexican Texts," *Journal of Women's History* 12, no. 3 (Autumn 2000): 69–92; Kathleen A. Deagan, "Sex, Status and Role in the Mestizaje of Spanish Colonial Florida," (PhD diss., University of Florida, 1974); Marisol de la Cadena, *Indigenous Mestizos: The Politics of Race and Culture in Cuzco, Peru, 1919–1991*, Latin American Otherwise: Languages, Empires, Nations (Durham, NC: Duke University Press, 2000); Milagros Palma, ed., *Simbólica de la Feminidad: La Mujer en el Imaginario Mítico Religioso de las Sociedades Indias y Mestizas*, Symposio del 40 Congreso Internacional de Americanistas, Amsterdam 1988, Colección 500 Años (Quito, Ecuador: Abya Yala, 1993).

  [7] In places such as Brazil, Colombia, and Cuba, the African presence and *mulato* discourses are effectively reduced to *mestizaje*. See Gilberto Freyre, *The Masters and the Slaves [Casa-Grande & Senzala]: A Study in the Development of Brazilian Civilization*, 4th ed., trans. Samuel Putnam

mixture of "white" Spanish and Portuguese with *Afro-descendentes* as *mulato/a* is part of the racialized hierarchical structures imposed by the larger colonizing project, which includes both *mulatez* and *mestizaje* among other racial classifications.

Second, *mestizaje* points to the historical condition of multiple cultural intermixtures. On the one hand, the adoption of *mestizaje* fruitfully led to an appreciation of rich and diverse Latina/o cultural sources: Indigenous, African, and European. On the other hand, such an affirmation is mitigated by the realization that it is because of the condition of racialized cultural *mestizaje* (intermixture) that Latinas/os experience social and political discrimination and economic marginalization particularly in the United States. In this sense, the adoption of *mestizaje* as an identifiable condition and category also unmasks the inherent cultural assimilationist and colonizing social and religious attitudes designed to discriminate against Latinas/os, rendering them perpetual outsiders.

Third, *mestizaje* appropriately conveys the dynamic contested nature of identities. It serves as a symbol for identifying the complex existential, fluid, in-between identity and social spaces inhabited by Latinas/os. This rich and complex human experience helps us envision the provisional character of identity descriptors and the unfinished character of identities as irreducible to facile and clearly defined identity notions. The deployment of *mestizaje* clearly demonstrates the dynamic and fluid character of Latina/o cultures, traditions, and identities, never fully fitting in pervasive airtight cultural frames.

(New York: Alfred A Knopf, 1946); Elisabeth Cunin, *Identidades a flor de piel: Lo 'negro' entre apariencias y pertenencias: categorías raciales y mestizaje en Cartagena (Colombia)* (Bogotá, Colombia: Instituto Colombiano de Antropología e Historia; Universidad de Los Andes; Instituto Francés de Estudios Andinos; Observatorio del Caribe Colombiano, 2003); Manuel Zapata Olivella, *La rebelión de los genes: El mestizaje americano en la sociedad futura* (Bogotá, Colombia: Ediciones Altamir, 1997).

And fourth, *mestizaje* refers to the complex socialized processes of code-switching—the "seamless" alternate use of two, three, or more cultures and traditions. It also points to disruptive linguistic practices of code-switching such as speaking in Spanglish. For Carmen Nanko-Fernández, these breaks with the protocol of monolingual grammar codes and syntax not only disrupt what is considered "proper speaking" but serve as vernacular theological sources.[8] These practices embody different epistemological frames for conceiving and understanding life and articulating the experiences of faith in God for Latinas/os.

These multiple meanings of *mestizaje* find their expression in religious traditions and theological articulations. *Mestizaje* operates as the key for unlocking the richness of Latina/o experiences of faith in God. Important limitations and challenges need to be considered when speaking about the condition, notion, and category of *mestizaje*.[9] This cultural experience marks the point of intersection between Latinas/os and their theologies' double synchronous act of deciphering and encrypting.

Deciphering entails the unraveling and unmasking of the multiple levels of intersection of oppression and the systemic exclusion rooted in culture and the racialization of Latinas/os. Deciphering refers to the ways Latina/o scholars engage in the complex processes of interpreting and translating the rich religious and cultural expressions of their communities. "Cultural" here refers to the very inescapable fabric of how a people view the world, understand reality, confront misery, and experience and

---

[8] See Carmen Nanko-Fernández, *Theologizing en Espanglish: Context, Community, and Ministry* (Maryknoll, NY: Orbis Books, 2010).

[9] Here I mean that *mestizaje* cannot be used without proper qualification of the meanings ascribed to it. It cannot be used as an all-encompassing category to speak for all of Latinas/os without proper acknowledgment of its multiple and historical racialized sources, internal contestations by different Latina/o actors, and inherent history as a category for the whitening of the population.

process pain and happiness. Encrypting has to do with re-codifying the resilient, persistent, even obstinate lived faith (*que no se da por vencida*) of Latina/o communities. Consider, for instance, how Latinas/os turn the Cartesian *cogito ergo sum* into *¡nosotros existimos y vivimos!*[10] In so doing they refuse to stop believing, because to cease to believe means to cease to live. Latina/o scholars have the onerous and exhilarating task of giving theological language to the people's everyday expressions and experiences of faith.

Mestizaje is not an innocent category; it is rooted in numerous, messy, violent, bloody, and often painful historical exchanges. It is a cipher, or symbol, that encompasses a complex set of intersecting forces (both positive and negative, emerging from both love and violence) that constitute Latina/o communities; it serves as a reservoir of theological wisdom, knowledge, and meaning.

Mestizaje: An Act of Collective (Re)Claiming

For Latina/o theologians the idea of *mestizaje* cuts across ethnocultural identities, histories, senses of peoplehood, and unique ways in which Latinas/os live and express their faith in God.[11] *Mestizaje* functions mnemonically because it brings to mind the complex and painful multiple strands of Latina/o history and the formation of Latina/o identities amid a context of conquest and violence. *Mestizaje* reveals disparate histor-

---

[10] Néstor Medina, "Tongue Twisters and Shibboleths: On Decolonial Gestures in Latin@ Theology," *Journal of Hispanic/Latina/o Theology* 18, no. 2 (June 2013): 13.

[11] One could say that by adopting *mestizaje* Latina/o theologians named themselves and their communities; reclaimed their history and agency; described the nature of their cultural and ethnic identity; gave language and content to their faith in God in the midst of discrimination and marginalization; provided a sense of coherence and unity against the dominant Anglo culture of the United States; challenged traditional approaches to theology; and reconfigured commonly accepted readings of the Bible text.

ical origins and their ongoing pervasive negative effects in
Latina/o communities. Historically *mestizos/as* emerged from
the cauldron of conquest and rape at the hands of Spaniards
and Portuguese, the cultural and ethnic destruction of the
native peoples of Abya Yala,[12] and the cultural decimation and
enslaving of the African populations brought to the continent
by European slave traders.

Mestizaje points beyond the original trauma and violence of
conquest. It unmasks a US history of expansionism, imperial attitudes, and a politics of interventionism that affected all of Latin
America in varying degrees and at different times.[13] Expansionism
and colonialism affected the Latina/o populations of Cuba and
Puerto Rico, for example. Interventionism affected Latinos/as of
El Salvador, Guatemala, and Colombia.[14] At a time of heightened
focus on immigration from Latin America, the act of claiming
mestizaje exposes how foreign policies, economic interests, and
corporations that use exploitative measures with no regard for
local customs and ecosystems are connected to and in many ways
responsible for migration.

Mestizaje exposes the racialized colonizing reasons for which
Latinas/os are absent from the historical imaginary of the United

---

[12] I am using a name ascribed to the region prior to the arrival of the
Spaniards and the colonizing act of changing the name to "America." Abya
Yala, Aztlán, and Turtle Island are some of the names given by Native peoples
to the region that today would include South, Central, and North America.

[13] Juan González, *Harvest of the Empire: A History of Latinos in
America* (New York: Penguin Books, 2000); Teresa Chávez Sauceda, "Race,
Religion, and la Raza: An Exploration of the Racialization of Latinos in
the United States and the Role of the Protestant Church," in *Protestantes
/ Protestants: Hispanic Christianity within Mainline Traditions*, ed. David
Maldonado Jr. (Nashville, TN: Abingdon, 1999), 177–93.

[14] See Seth Motel and Eileen Patten, "The 10 Largest Hispanic Origin
Groups: Characteristics, Rankings, Top Countries," Pew Research Center,
June 27, 2012, https://www.pewresearch.org/hispanic/2012/06/27/the-
10-largest-hispanic-origin-groups-characteristics-rankings-top-counties/.

States. For example, the broken promises of the 1848 Guadalupe-Hidalgo Treaty have long contributed to discriminatory policies and practices targeting Latinos/as, particularly Mexican Americans in the Southwest.[15] As the late Virgilio Elizondo would say, *mestizaje* marks systemic racialized dynamics and discrimination.[16] Such dynamics of exclusion are evident in the underrepresentation of Latinos/as at every level of government and in ecclesial positions of leadership among Catholics, mainline Protestants, and Pentecostals,[17] despite the fact that they constitute a significant number of these communities. Among Catholics, for instance, Latinas/os represent the fastest-growing segment of the population.[18] It also helps explain why Latinas/os—though encompassing almost 20 percent of the total population—continue to be overrepresented (33 percent as of 2016) in the prison population of the country.[19]

Finally, *mestizaje* allows Latinas/os to interrogate their own cultural matrices, unmask the ways in which oppression and discrimination take place within their communities, and dismantle the ways that Latinas/os reproduce the rationality of colonization. This means that *nuestros propios encubrimientos*, that is, our own cover-ups, need

---

[15] For a critical commentary on the treaty and its impact, see Richard Griswold del Castillo, *The Treaty of Guadalupe Hidalgo: A Legacy of Conflict* (Norman, OK: University of Oklahoma Press, 1990).

[16] See Elizondo, "Mestizaje as a Locus of Theological Reflection," 358–74.

[17] For fuller discussions on the multiple ways in which Latina/o Catholics have historically been discriminated against, see Jean-Pierre Ruiz, *Reading from the Edges: The Bible and People on the Move* (Maryknoll, NY: Orbis Books, 2011). For a fuller understanding of the history of Latina/o mainline Protestants in their huge diversity, see Maldonado, *Protestantes / Protestants*.

[18] Pew Research Center, *The Shifting Religious Identity of Latinos in the United States*, Religion and Public Life Project (2014), https://www.pewresearch.org/religion/2014/05/07/the-shifting-religious-identity-of-latinos-in-the-united-states/

[19] See "Inmate Ethnicity," Federal Bureau of Prisons, https://www.bop.gov/about/statistics/statistics_inmate_race.jsp

to be identified and interrogated.[20] Our complicated histories challenge romanticized portrayals of *mestizaje*. The colonial past has left its mark. Latinas/os have inherited a history of internalized and racialized hierarchies and strife. This past still shapes the way we establish our social structures, build our traditions, and imagine our intraethnic, cultural, and religious differences. Many in our communities still feel the effects of discrimination inflicted because of our indigenous and African ancestry. Thus, the different ancestral and cultural strands celebrated in *mestizaje* must also move us to challenge and dismantle the assumptions behind internalized racial and ideological divisions that organize and classify Latinas/os hierarchically. These divisions often take place on the basis of color, language, nationality, and culture.

One contribution of *mestizaje* to discourses of identity, ethnicity, and race is its capacity to connect Latinas/os to the broader human family. History teaches us that processes of intermixture have marked human existence.[21] The norm has never been racial purity. Intermixture has affected many societies at different points and in different ways, and continues to preoccupy many today, particularly in large multicultural urban centers.[22] Meanwhile, the fictitious and arbitrary division of humanity by races has been scientifically discredited by the genome project. Since the

[20] Medina, *Mestizaje: (Re)Mapping*; Gloria Anzaldúa, *Borderlands / La Frontera: The New Mestiza* (San Francisco: Aunt Lute Books, 1987); María Pilar Aquino, "The Collective 'Dis-Covery' of Our Own Power: Latina American Feminist Theology," in *Hispanic / Latino Theology: Challenge and Promise*, ed. Ada María Isasi-Díaz and Fernando Segovia (Minneapolis: Fortress Press, 1996), 240–60.

[21] Virgilio Elizondo, "The New Humanity of the Americas," in *Beyond Borders: The Writings of Virgilio Elizondo and Friends*, ed. Timothy Matovina (Maryknoll, NY: Orbis Books, 2000), 272–77; Jacques Ruffié, *De la biologie à la culture*, Novelle bibliothèque scientifique (Paris: Flammarion, 1976).

[22] Jacques Audinet, *The Human Face of Globalization: From Multicultural to Mestizaje*, trans. Frances Dal Chele (Lanham, MD: Rowman & Littlefield, 2004).

middle of the twentieth century epigenetics and the surrounding environment have been used to explain phenotypical differences among human groups.[23] Also, I would argue that conversations, which previously focused on race, have now shifted to focus on cultures. Too many speak of "culture" using language similar to that used in the eighteenth, nineteenth, and twentieth centuries in reference to race. What we are increasingly experiencing is a global shift toward the racialized culturalization of peoples. *Mestizaje* gives us a glance into human history as marked by the violence of empire, colonization, and migration that resulted from cultural intermixture and miscegenation.

Those who see themselves as *mestizos/as* simultaneously embody, unmask, and are victims of the colonialism of European self-perception and the European intellectual tradition. For Latinas/os, *mestizaje* accomplished more than just the recognition of the condition of human mixture. As part of the complex set of castes that were created during the Spanish and Portuguese colonial societies and in light of the present pervasive racialized hierarchy of ethnic and cultural groups, *mestizaje* redefines our understanding of racialization and intermixture. *Mestizaje* challenges the colonialism of pigmentation or pigmentocracy. On the one hand, *mestizaje* dismantles ideas that the lighter the skin, the less mixed (the purer) a person is. Today we know that lighter skin does not point to racial "purity." On the other hand, *mestizaje* shows that inherited ideological notions and constructions of "whiteness" are predicated on artificial and arbitrary phenotypical claims. In the colonial matrix the violated "other" "colored" skins are the other side (the underside) of "whiteness."[24]

---

[23] See Roger Highfield, "DNA Survey Finds All Humans Are 99.9pc the Same," *Telegraph*, Monday, June 6, 2016, https://www.telegraph.co.uk/news/worldnews/northamerica/usa/1416706/DNA-survey-finds-all-humans-are-99.9pc-the-same.html

[24] Although not explicitly related to the idea of whiteness, discussions

Let me state unequivocally the following: *mestizaje* is not the romantic feat of ethnocultural strands providentially coming together producing something new. Such an affirmation would leave unchallenged the imperial pretensions of Europe,[25] the negative violent effects of colonization,[26] the erasure and silencing of indigenous peoples and Afro-descendants,[27] the violence against women, and the undergirding theological edifice that supported colonization. Instead, *mestizaje* entails a historiographical revisioning, a problematizing of notions of identities, and a redrafting of our theological frames. In many ways, it is these characteristics that make *mestizaje* simultaneously both a promising and useful category and a contested and risky one.

Mestizaje helps unmask the fallacy behind inherited sanitized notions of history from the vantage point of the victor and retrieves the underside of that history. The story always looks different from the side of the vanquished. In addition, *mestizaje* clarifies and frees notions of identity by encompassing the complex and messy processes of culturalization. Ethnic and cultural identities are never finished products, nor are they airtight, clearly defined, and self-contained. They are fluid, porous, changeable, and involved in constant processes of exchange and intermixture. Moreover, identity formations include processes of social power struggle and resistance, economic survival, interethnic violence, and contested

---

of modernity carry the same operative racialized axis between modernity and its underside. See Enrique Dussel, *The Underside of Modernity: Apel, Ricoeur, Rorty, Taylor, and the Philosophy of Liberation*, ed. and trans. Eduardo Mendieta (Atlantic Highlands, NJ: Humanities Press, 1996); Paul Gilroy, *The Black Atlantic: Modernity and Double Consciousness* (Cambridge, MA: Harvard University Press, 1993).

[25] Medina, "Tongue Twisters and Shibboleths."

[26] Néstor Medina, "The Religious Psychology of *Mestizaje*: Gómez Suárez de Figueroa or Garcilaso de la Vega," *Pastoral Psychology* 57 (2008): 115–24.

[27] Medina, *Mestizaje: (Re)Mapping.*

processes of cultural construction. In *mestizaje,* one cannot separate the oppressive colonial power matrix from the struggles and resistance of people.

Finally, the deployment of *mestizaje* by Latina/o theologians and scholars reconfigures theological methodology, which include defining how to begin theological reflection and what to include as theological subjects.[28] Pursuant to this end, in the following section, I discuss some of the ways in which Latina/o adoptions of *mestizaje* yield important theological insights. More specifically, I embrace the capacity of *mestizaje* to offer a unique angle of vision, opting for its cultural dimension as a fundamental *locus theologicus.*[29]

Mestizaje: Reframing the Theological Task

A discussion on *mestizaje* would be incomplete if I did not engage the religious/theological aspect of these debates. Just as all theologies are historically grounded, contextually constructed, and culturally conditioned, so too are Latina/o theological claims on *mestizaje.* Latina/o theological and methodological claims decenter traditional dominant theologies. They show that those theologies embody the ways Western Europeans and Anglo North Atlantic scholars have responded to issues and challenges in their context. Theological claims and approaches from the Global North often leave unchallenged and unaddressed the history of conquest, colonization, and oppression experienced by the majority world. The specific experiences of Latin Americans and Latinas/os are brought to light with *mestizaje.* By reinterpreting their historical heritage of intermixture and conquest, and by reclaiming the vantage point of *mestizaje,* Latinas/os reconfigure the theological task and offer new ways for thinking theologi-

---

[28] Medina, *Mestizaje: (Re)Mapping,* 126–30.

[29] For a discussion of what I mean by the cultural, see Néstor Medina, *Christianity, Empire and the Spirit* (Leiden: Brill, 2018).

cally about a people's experience of faith in God. In what follows I briefly show some of the insights we can glean from the Latina/o theological project in three areas: (1) a new vision of humanity, (2) culture as a critical theological component, and (3) popular religion as a site of people's theological articulation.

A New Vision of Humanity

According to Virgilio Elizondo, *mestizaje* reveals the providential growing creation of a new humanity in the Americas.[30] This coming together recognizes the history of violence, culturecide, and othercide,[31] but it also bears the potential for ethnoracial and cultural coexistence. My intention is not to undermine the rich multicultural, multilingual, and multiethnic presences in Latin America and among Latinas/os in the United States and Canada. Rather, my affirmation points to the celebration of the multiple and complex racialized ethnocultural streams that have contributed to the formation of Latin American and Latina/o identities. *Mestizaje* challenges us to interrogate inherited racialized hierarchical schemes because they contribute to the impoverishment of our humanity. It is impossible, however, to pretend to remove social hierarchies (class, color, race, gender, sexual orientation) without critically engaging their historical legacy and baggage. In this sense, reclaiming *mestizaje* helps reclaim the human condition of pain, brokenness, beauty, and love simultaneously, though

---

[30] Elizondo, "The New Humanity of the Americas," 272–77.

[31] Here I am taking a different stance from those of José Vasconcelos and Virgilio Elizondo, among others, who adopted a romanticized view of *mestizaje*. See my positions in Medina, *Mestizaje: (Re)Mapping*, and in "The Religious Psychology of *Mestizaje*." For a discussion of some of the scholars involved in these debates, see Jorge A. Aquino, "*Mestizaje*: The Latina/o Religious Imaginary in the North American Racial Crucible," in *The Wiley Blackwell Companion to Latino/a Theology*, ed. Orlando Espín (West Sussex, UK: Wiley Blackwell, 2015), 281–311.

expressed in myriad ways. Thus, *mestizaje* marks our racialized ethnocultural human interconnectedness. Yet there is no one thing we can call *mestizaje*. Rather, there are multiple spaces of ethnocultural and identity negotiations, historical intersections of violence, exchanges and cross-fertilizations that lead to the further proliferation of identities and ethnocultural affiliations.[32]

The elevation of *mestizaje* as a *locus theologicus*, a strategic move that provides an interpretive frame, allows us to explore three interconnected insights. First, the humanity of Jesus is reclaimed as *mestiza*. The incarnation, writes Luis Pedraja, can be understood as the *mestizo* (and for him also *mulato)* moment of divine human enfleshment.[33] But interpreting the incarnation as *mestiza* does not merely illustrate a superficial forceful blending and mixing of the divine and the human. It opens new avenues for understanding the human-divine relationship by which the Triune God, in the incarnation, elevates the ethnoculturally conditioned humanity of Mary as site and locus of this new relation. And in the no less ethnoculturally conditioned *mestizo* Jesus,[34] God opens a new path for reorienting our understanding of humanity. Furthermore, it is important to note that our humanity cannot be lived outside of the cultural dimension. Finally, interpreting Jesus as *mestizo* broadens our understanding of the *communicatio idiomatum*, bringing to light the collaboration between the human and divine in the construction of a new humanity able to reflect the divine imaging. To view Jesus within his ethnocultural ecosystem resonates with the communal nature of the Triune God. Jesus as *mestizo* must be understood as the celebration of the materiality of life in collaboration with the divine.

---

[32] Medina, *Mestizaje: (Re)Mapping,* chap. 5.

[33] Luis G. Pedraja, *Jesus Is My Uncle: Christology from a Hispanic Perspective* (Nashville, TN: Abingdon Press, 1999), 82–84.

[34] See Virgilio Elizondo, *Galilean Journey: The Mexican-American Promise* (Maryknoll, NY: Orbis Books, 1983).

The second insight is closely connected to this consideration of the *mestizo* humanity of Jesus, insofar as it opens up the possibilities for articulating a new understanding of human-based intermixture. If indeed the incarnation embodies *mestizo(a)*-like collaboration between the human and divine at the cultural level, then *mestizaje* also serves as the pattern for human existence and coexistence among cultural communities. Again, it would be a mistake to romanticize Jesus' historical existence. He lived the pain, the sorrow, and the discrimination that he and many others experienced because of their social status, cultural background, and the "moral" standing ascribed to them by the dominant imperial establishment. Yet it was from within this experience of human social cross-fertilization, cultural intermixture, and struggle for justice and equality that his *mestizo*-interconnectedness with God gained new dimensions. He paved the way to break with all the arbitrarily prescribed social, economic, political, and cultural boundaries that seek to prevent many from reaching the fullness of humanity. The *mestizo* humanity of Jesus marks the intentional undoing of the inherited damaging social stereotypes and culturalized ethnoracial markers that separate human collectives. The *mestiza* humanity of Jesus also suggests that only by coming together, that is, by *mestizizing,* can humans appropriately reflect their divine imaging, reach full humanity, and learn to coexist—without forgetting the sinful legacy of their violent history.

The third insight stems from an affirmation of the importance and central role of cultural *mestizizing*. Historically speaking, humanity has grown and communities have been formed at the intersection and intermixture of histories, ethnicities, and cultures. The insight is that there is no such thing as a universal idea of what it means to be "human." *Mestizaje* offers an alternative understanding of human communities, always formed in the cauldron of contextuality and local cultural conditioning. The cultural dimension is not an accidental feature here but an essential part of the ways in which communities live their humanity, express their faith in God concretely, and collaborate with the divine in the perpetuation and protection of life in all of its historically grounded and culturally conditioned character.

None of these three insights promotes the emergence of a single cosmic race or global identity. Rather, *mestizaje* marks the point of redefinition of our understanding of human cultural and identity boundaries. *Mestizaje* renders attempts to essentialize and racialize cultural and identity categories woefully insufficient!

The Cultural as Critical Theological Site

The affirmation of *mestizaje* points to the celebration of the cultural dimension of human persons as the irreducible site of human activity and interaction. What is meant by "cultural" here is celebrated not as a series of elite social tools, entitlements, or a specific set of rules for human interaction. Rather, what is "cultural," as mentioned earlier, refers to the inescapable fabric of how people view the world, understand reality, confront misery, and experience and process both pain and happiness. The "cultural" corresponds to that open-ended, fluid, and linked series of codes and segments of codes by which people make sense of life, interact with each other and the world, and approach the divine.[35]

Cultures constitute the frameworks within which different communities conceive and interact with the divine and express their faith in God. Latinas/os, claims Orlando Espín, can express their faith only in culturally conditioned Latina/o ways.[36] They also cannot engage in theological reflection by suspending their cultural traditions. Rather, their theological reflections are culturally shaped

---

[35] For a discussion on what I mean by "cultural," see Medina, *Christianity, Empire and the Spirit*, 13–50.

[36] Orlando O. Espín, *The Faith of the People: Theological Reflections on Popular Catholicism* (Maryknoll, NY: Orbis Books, 1997), 94–95.

and conditioned. The celebration of the *mestizo* incarnation as fundamentally cultural, as discussed above, points to the celebration of the cultural as the *conditio sine qua non* of theological reflection. This understanding of the intricate connection between theological reflection and culture goes beyond elementary contextual reflections on theology insofar as it makes manifest the deep conditioning power and effect of one's cultural traditions on all aspects of life.

As a critical category, *mestizaje* leads us to celebrate Latina/o cultural traditions and embrace specific epistemological sources (such as fiesta, la quinceañera, las posadas, and other customs). It includes the particular ways that Latinas/os construct theological knowledge *en y de conjunto*. Epistemologically speaking, *mestizaje* embraces theological knowledge that "comes from the community (*en conjunto*) and belongs to the community (*de conjunto*)."[37] In short, *mestizaje* allows us to reclaim those long-standing traditions and sources of knowledge that as of yet remain absent in traditional approaches to theology (e.g., orality,[38] dreams, stories,[39] and even gossip[40]). Here the stance against racialized, discriminatory, sexist,

---

[37] Néstor Medina and Neomi DeAnda, "Convivencias: What Have We Learned? Toward a Latina/o Ecumenical Theology," in *Building Bridges, Doing Justice: Constructing a Latino/a Ecumenical Theology*, ed. Orlando Espín (Maryknoll, NY: Orbis Books, 2009), 185.

[38] Ana María Pineda, "The Oral Tradition of a People: Forjadora de Rostro y Corazón," in *Hispanic / Latino Theology: Challenge and Promise*, ed. Ada María Isasi-Díaz and Segovia Fernando (Minneapolis: Fortress Press, 1996), 104–17; Néstor Medina, "Orality and Context in a Hermeneutical Key: Toward a Latina/o Canadian Pentecostal Life-Narrative Hermeneutics," *PentecoStudies* 14, no. 1 (2015): 97–123.

[39] Although not strictly theological, the work of Milagros Palma in Nicaragua illustrates the rich fabric of stories-cuentos and their central cultural and religious role among communities. See Palma, *Simbólica de la Feminidad*; Milagros Palma, *La mujer es puro cuento: simbólica mítico-religiosa de la feminidad aborigen y mestiza*, 2d ed. (Quito, Ecuador: Abya Yala, 1996).

[40] Neomi DeAnda, "Reflections on God, Life and Gossip in Tele-

and gendered elements within Latina/o theology must be high-lighted. *Mestizaje* charts a new trajectory of theological sources and reclaims indigenous, African, and Latin American intellectual reservoirs that do not always draw on the Enlightenment.[41] Those are not just potential venues but represent actual epistemologies— a great multicultural, multilingual, multiethnic cloud of witnesses that can help us in reorienting, re-creating, and reimagining the theological task.

Popular Religion as a Site of People's Theological Articulation

Latina/o theologians highlight the importance of paying attention to popular religions and popular religious expressions. The corpus of Latina/o theologies reflects how these scholars have understood the intersection between the faith experiences of a people and their expressions. Scholars such as Orlando Espín, Roberto Goizueta, and Virgilio Elizondo have insisted repeat-edly that Latina/o popular religious traditions and expressions are legitimately carriers of the people's profound sense of faith in God and of divine disclosure.[42] They insist that we find the

---

novelas," electronic *Journal of Hispanic/Latino Theology* (2009).

[41] These ancestors include voices such as Felipe Guamán Poma de Ayala, Mama Chimpu Oclo, Garcilaso de la Vega, José de San Martín, Tupac Amarú, José Gabriel Condorcanqui, José Carlos Mariáteguí, José Fernández Retamar, José Martí, Che Guevara, Rigoberta Menchú, Sor Juana Inés de la Cruz, María Ana Águeda de San Ignacio, Antonio de Montesinos, Hatuey, Los Mambises de Cuba y los Yoruba de Brazil, Chilam Balam, Popul Vuh, y el Memorial de Sololá. All of these voices together with indigenous, *Afro-descendente*, and multicultural other communities that make up Latinas/os and Latin Americans, with all of their tensions and contradictions, can contribute to this epistemological task.

[42] Orlando Espín has dedicated much of his theological work to help us understand the intricate and dynamic world of popular religious tradi-tions. See Orlando O. Espín: *Idol & Grace: Our Traditioning and Subversive*

divine at work in the popular, that is, in the people's religious activities. In making this argument, Latina/o theologians are not merely stating the obvious, namely, that there is no such thing as a single and culturally neutral expression of Christianity. Rather, these theologians affirm that popular religious traditions, expressions, and practices of the people—which at one point were labeled syncretistic and corrupted or were even demonized—are legitimate conveyors of theological knowledge. Our theological reflection ought to start and end with the religious expressions of the people.

We have already seen how *mestizaje* offers theology a distinct point of view, a category of analysis, a historical interpretive frame, and a condition of ethnocultural intermixture. But how do *mestizaje* and theology connect with popular religions and popular religious traditions and expressions? Though the answer requires much elaboration, I offer an initial response: popular religious traditions embody in their multiple diverse expressions the ways in which people think theologically as they engage in the day-to-day complex, multilayered processes of *mestizization*, including religious intermixture. Latina/o communities' religious symbols, practices, customs, and traditions display the inherited deep-seated amalgam of indigenous and African religious elements and Spanish and Portuguese expressions of Christianity. In particular, today's expression of Latina/o Christian faith attests to the historical

---

Hope (Maryknoll, NY: Orbis Books, 2014); *The Faith of the People*; "Popular Religion as an Epistemology (of Suffering)," *Journal of Hispanic/ Latino Theology* 2, no. 2 (November 1994): 55–78; "Popular Catholicism: Alienation or Hope?" in *Hispanic / Latino Theology: Challenge and Promise*, ed. Ada María Isasi-Díaz and Fernando F. Segovia (Minneapolis: Fortress Press, 1996), 307–24; "Tradition and Popular Religion: *An Understanding of The* Sensus Fidelium," in *Mestizo Christianity: Theology from the Latino Perspective*, ed. Arturo J. Bañuelas (Maryknoll, NY: Orbis Books, 1995), 146–74.

violence of the conquest and the present experience of racialized social, cultural, political, and economic discrimination. These expressions can appropriately be identified as *mestizo* popular religious traditions and theologies.

The religious traditions of the people do not remain stagnant. These traditions have changed enormously through different periods of colonial societies, wars of independence, periods of nationalization, US expansionism, and present shifting global contexts. Indeed, today's popular religious expressions are the result of complex processes of racialized, contextual, ethnic, cultural, sociopolitical, and theological intermixture. Latinas/os weave, that is, they *mestizize*, their own cultural elements and traditions, including their historical baggage of violence, as they live and experience marginalization and discrimination. In this way, popular religious traditions can legitimately be called *mestizas* since they are simultaneously expressions of the deepest devotions of the people, collective stances of resistance, and lived theological affirmations.

To state the obvious, let us not romanticize! We can say that the adoption of *mestizaje* helps us envision popular religious expressions that reflect messy, painful, and contested social contexts. Popular religious expressions embody inherited forms of violence and the realities of pain and suffering. They also reflect the dreams and future aspirations toward the construction of a better world for persons, families, and communities. *Mestizaje* helps illuminate how it is that as persons experience life—in all life's tensions and contradictions—they also theologize. How persons come to understand the divine emerges from their experiences of pain, sorrow, happiness, pleasure, celebration, violence, and discrimination. It is in the process of negotiating and making sense of their existence at the levels of the racialized, political, economic, social, cultural, and biological that Latinas/os encounter, interact with, and reflect on the divine.

Going Forward

The theological articulation of *mestizaje* points to the radical intersection of cultural, racial-ethnic, gender, and identity issues. It unmasks the non-innocence of all processes of theological reflection. It also unburies the historical skeletons in the closet of traditional theological discourses as it carves out new social, theological, ideological, and identity spaces for reclaiming the multiple sources of our complex identities. *Mestizaje* exposes the fundamental quality of theological reflection as emerging from the incarnated and deeply cultural character of faith. In other words, it is as people live and express their faith in God that they engage in the radical, uneven, unfinished, and continuing processes of *mestizization*. Latinas/os are creating disruptive shibboleths that create new tools and new spaces for thinking of the divine from the perspective of our cultural traditions.

As we imagine and work toward another possible world, it is important to reemphasize that *mestizaje* is not an abstract romantic category. *Mestizaje* brings with it dissonance, disconnectedness, and unresolved ambiguities and tensions. It is a category grounded in history that cannot be sanitized. Beyond a simple coming together of elements, it includes inherently the dynamics of contestation between disparate origins, traditions, religions, and cultures. In short, *mestizaje* corresponds to the day-to-day incarnated reality that people confront where their faith plays a crucial role in challenging inherited worldviews and in providing a sense of coherence and hope.

5

Playing en los Márgenes

Lo Popular as *Locus Theologicus*

Carmen M. Nanko-Fernández

In Latin@́ worldviews, where relationships between sacred and secular are often porous, the faiths of the people find expression in material culture, and in a variety of media, practices, and performances that constitute lo popular, literally that which is of the people, with origins in the ordinary.[1] A number of Latin@́ theologians have done pioneering work establishing popular Catholicism as

---

[1] Words and expressions in Spanish are not italicized unless they appear as such in direct quotations. Spanish is not a "foreign" language in the USA. *Galego* is italicized. At times sentences include multiple languages, part of the code-switching that marks daily interactions. I created @, the 'at' symbol (el arroba) *with* an acute accent mark. I borrow the use of @ as a gender inclusive suffix, which at the same time destabilizes gender polarities. I add the acute accent (@́) to signify the fluidity of language, culture, and identity, and to emphasize the role of location and situatedness in theology done latinamente. I develop these themes in my book *Theologizing en Espanglish: Context, Community and Ministry* (Maryknoll, NY: Orbis Books, 2010). On lo popular see pages 13-17 in Carmen M. Nanko-Fernández, "Lo Cotidiano as *Locus Theologicus,*" *The Wiley Blackwell Companion to Latinoax Theology* (2nd edition), Orlando O. Espín, ed. (Hoboken, NJ: John Wiley and Sons, LTD, 2023).

locus theologicus.[2] Popular culture as a source for theologizing latinamente remains ripe for further development,[3] as does the retrieval of
forgotten antecedents from the complex matrices of hispanidad.[4]

---

[2] Among the classic texts see, for example, Virgilio Elizondo, *Guada-lupe: Mother of the New Creation* (Maryknoll, NY: Orbis Books, 1997);
Orlando O. Espín, *The Faith of the People: Theological Reflections on Popular Catholicism* (Maryknoll, NY: Orbis Books, 1997); Alex García-Rivera, *St. Martín de Porres: The Little Stories and the Semiotics of* Culture (Mary-knoll, NY: Orbis Books, 1995); Roberto S. Goizueta, *Caminemos con Jesús: Toward a Hispanic/Latino Theology of Accompaniment* (Maryknoll, NY: Orbis Books, 1995); Jeanette Rodriguez, *Our Lady of Guadalupe: Faith and Empowerment among Mexican American Women* (Austin, TX: University of Texas Press, 1994).

[3] See, for example, the following articles in the electronic *Journal of Hispanic/Latino Theology*: Gilberto Cavazos-González, OFM, "'You don't pay me enough:' La Salvadora Kenotica in US Film and Television" (2009); Neomi De Anda, "¡Dame chisme! dame chocolate! Reflections on God, Life and Gossip in Telenovelas" (2009); Cecilia González-Andrieu, "Theological Aesthetics and the Recovery of Silenced Voices" (2008); Jacqueline Hidalgo, "Scripting Latinidad: Re/Defining Textual Selves and Worlds in the Age of MySpace" (2009). Carmen Nanko-Fernández, "Turning Those Others' Cheeks: Racial Martyrdom and the Re-Integration of Major League Base-ball," in *Gods, Games, and Globalization*, ed. Arthur Remillard and Rebecca T. Alpert (Macon, GA: Mercer University Press, 2019), 239–62; and Carmen M. Nanko-Fernández, "Safe @ Home y en diáspora: the Sanctification of Roberto Clemente," *Aztlán: A Journal of Chicano Studies* 47(1) (2022), 167–177. Anthony Pinn and Benjamín Valentín, eds., *Creating Ourselves: African Amer-icans and Hispanic Americans on Popular Culture and Religious Expression* (Durham, NC: Duke University Press, 2009).

[4] Examples of Latin@ historical retrievals include Claudio M. Burgaleta, *José de Acosta (1540–1600): His Life and Thought* (Chicago: Loyola Press, 1999); Neomi De Anda, "Images of God, Imago Dei and God's Relationship with Humanity through the Image of Mary's Breast Milk: A Focus on Sor María Anna Águeda De San Ignacio (1695–1756)" (PhD diss., Loyola University Chicago, 2011); Miguel H. Díaz, *Queer God de Amor* (New York, NY: Fordham University Press, 2022); Raúl Gómez-Ruiz, *Mozarabs, Hispanics, and the Cross* (Maryknoll, NY: Orbis Books, 2007); Jean-Pierre Ruiz and Carmen Nanko-Fernández, "Dialogues in the

Situating the Interpreter

I am an Hispan@ hybrid from the Bronx, New York. *Galego* and *castellano* were the two languages my immigrant maternal abuelo e abuela brought with them in their journey from Galicia en España to Cuba to Nueva York. In one generation la lengua gallega was gone, and Spanish and English became the new bilingualism in my mother's familia in the United States. My dad taught us to play baseball, and we learned from him that fair play meant access to a level field for all, especially those kids on the margins of playgrounds. I grew up at Yankee Stadium believing that one day I would be a catcher for the "Bronx Bombers," and thanks to mi tía's job in public relations with the team, our familia was traditioned into Yankee Universe, though we were ecumenical New Yorkers because our fandom embraced the crosstown Mets. New York baseball provided a powerful and emotional connection to home during the trauma and aftermath of the events of 11 September 2001, and béisbol furnished a critical lens that allowed me to break my scholarly silence on those experiences a decade later.[5]

When I got "traded" to Chicago, I dealt with my homesickness

Margins: The Biblia De Alba and the Future of Catholic-Jewish Understanding," in *Toward the Future: Essays on Catholic-Jewish Relations in Memory of Rabbi León Klenicki*, ed. Celia Deutsch, Eugene Fisher, and A. James Rudin (New York: Paulist Press, 2013), 35–51; Jean-Pierre Ruiz, "The Bible and the Exegesis of Empire: Reading Christopher Columbus's *El libro de las profecías*," in *Readings from the Edges: The Bible and People on the Move* (Maryknoll, NY: Orbis Books, 2011), 123–35; Jean-Pierre Ruiz, "Cardinal Francisco Ximénez de Cisneros and Bartolomé de las Casas, the 'Procurator and Universal Protector of All Indians in the Indies,'" *Journal of Hispanic/Latino Theology* 9 (February 2002): 60–77; Jean-Pierre Ruiz, *Revelation in the Vernacular* (New York, NY: Fordham University Press, 2023).

[5] Carmen M. Nanko-Fernández, "Ordinary Theologies, Extraordinary Circumstances: Baseball at the Intersections of Faith and Popular Culture," in *Recovering 9/11 in New York*, eds. Robert Fanuzzi and Michael Wolfe (Newcastle, UK: Cambridge Scholars Press, 2014), 68–87.

and disorientation by heading to the ballpark to witness former Yankee José Contreras pitch his first home game with his new team, the White Sox. For me this was a means to survival, a place to reorient, and an act of solidarity between two uprooted urban Hispanic migrant workers in an alien land. In a certain sense I am situated within la iglesia de béisbol, it is part of mi vida cotidiana as a schoolyard player, a fan, and a theologian. Baseball is about home, familia, childhood dreams, and béisbol is about resistance, playing in the margins, and theologizing en espanglish. I resonate with the words of Pope Francisco when he addressed his hometown soccer team because, like him, the sport I grew up on and my hometown teams also "forman parte de mi identidad cultural."[6]

Retrieving Béisbol?

Hanging in the museum at the National Baseball Hall of Fame in Cooperstown, New York, is a reproduction of a miniature from las *Cantigas de Santa María*, a thirteenth-century manuscript collection of four hundred and twenty poems of Marian devotion with thousands of accompanying illuminations and musical annotations.[7] This image is the earliest portrayal of a bat and ball

---

[6] Words of Pope Francisco, on the occasion of the Vatican visit of his favorite soccer team, San Lorenzo de Almagro, following its first ever championship at the prestigious South American club soccer tournament *Copa Libertadores*. Francisco explained that this was his family's team, the result of a long association with the athletic club that sponsors it. Reported in "El papa saludó al San Lorenzo: 'Son parte de su identidad cultural,'" *Marca*, August 20, 2014, https://www.marca.com/2014/08/20/futbol/futbol_internacional/argentina/1408529730.html

[7] The *Cantigas de Santa María* are preserved in four codices of varying lengths, some with illustrated miniatures, others not. One codex, originally in the Cathedral at Toledo, is now at the Biblioteca Nacional de Madrid, two codices are in the Biblioteca del Monasterio de El Escorial, one codex is in the Biblioteca Nazionale in Florence, Italy. For a brief

game in Iberia and may well be one of the ancestors of baseball.[8]
This panel is the second of six illustrating a song known by number,
Cantiga 42. The caption, "*Como iogavan a pelota os mancebos en un
prado,*" explains "how young men are playing ball in a meadow."[9]
It depicts two sets of actions: in the background, what appear to

overview of each codex, see Gonzalo Menéndez Pidal, "Los Manuscritos
de las Cantigas: Cómo se Elaboró Miniatura Alfonsí," *Boletín de la Real
Academia de la Historia* (1962): 30–35, http://www.cervantesvirtual.com/
nd/ark:/59851/bmc1c2h5 ; and Connie L. Scarborough, Introduction to
*Songs of Holy Mary of Alfonso X, The Wise: A Translation of the Cantigas
de Santa Maria,* trans. Kathleen Kulp-Hill (Tempe, AZ: Arizona Center
for Medieval and Renaissance Studies, 2000), xxiii–xxiv. For a sense of the
magnitude of the *Cantigas,* see the Centre for the Study of the *Cantigas
de Santa Maria* of Oxford University (http://csm.mml.ox.ac.uk) hosting
the *Cantigas de Santa Maria* Database. This bilingual site is in English and
galego. Please note that the spelling of the name María varies by publication,
with some rendering the name without the acute accent.

8 For overviews on the history of ball playing in Spain, see Daniel
García García-Maroto and Sergio García González, "Patrimonio Histórico
Español del Juego y del Deporte: *Las Cantigas de Santa María,*" Museo del
Juego (2014), http://museodeljuego.org/investigaci%c3%b3n/patrimonio-
hist%c3%b3rico/biblioteca/cantigas-de-santa-maria/ ; Manuel Hernández
Vázquez, "El Juego Deportivo en la España Cristiana," Museo del Juego,
Spain, 23–26, http://museodeljuego.org/historia/edad-media/j-d-
espa%c3%b1a-cristiana/el-juego-deportivo-en-la-espa%c3%b1a-cristiana/
9 To read Cantiga 42, with narrative in English and miniature captions
in *galego* and English, see "CSM Number: 42, 'The Ring on the Finger of
the Virgin's Statue,'" *Cantigas de Santa Maria* Database, https://csm.
mml.ox.ac.uk/index.php?narOption=all&p=poemdata_view&rec=42.
To see the digitized miniatures (T-I-1_fol-061V.jpg), music (T-I-1_fol-
060R.jpg, T-I-1_fol-060V.jpg), and read the verses (T-I-1_fol-060V.jpg,
T-I-1_fol-061R.jpg) in medieval *galego,* go to: XLII, *Cantigas de Santa
María,* Códice rico, Real Biblioteca del Monasterio de San Lorenzo
de El Escorial, 128-131, https://rbdigital.realbiblioteca.es/s/rbme/
item/11337#?c=&m=&s=&cv=&xywh=-3010%2C-313%2C9763%2C6240.
To read the most recent English translation in a comprehensive volume, see
"42," in Kathleen Kulp-Hill, trans., *Songs of Holy Mary,* 55–56.

be three fielders attempt to catch a ball in the air, and in the foreground a pitcher tosses a ball to a batter in a stance more familiar to baseball than cricket.

The verses of this song establish this scene as a detail in a miracle story about "how the postulant placed the ring on the finger of the statue of Holy Mary, and the statue curved its finger around it."[10] The setting is a town square, in Germany, where a temporarily relocated statue of Mary sits while her church undergoes renovation. In the park within the plaza, local folk took their pleasure and enjoyed playing ball, "which is the favorite game of all young men."[11] One of the young men who comes out to play ball is in love, wearing a ring from his beloved. In order not to damage the ring he places it on the finger of the statue and makes a profession of fidelity to Mary, pledging to love no other woman but her. He is stunned when the statue curls her finger around the ring, a miracle that inspires the town folk to encourage him to enter the monastery at Claraval.[12] The narrative continues with the fickle young man forgetting his promise to Mary; at the urging of his parents, he marries his beloved. That night in the nuptial bed, Mary visits him twice in dreams and chastises him as a liar: "*Ai, meu falss' e mentiral!*" She inserts herself between the sleeping bride and groom, and insists he honor his pledge by leaving his wife to go with her, lest he "suffer mortal anguish."[13] The fifth panel in the series depicts Mary pulling the unclothed young man out of bed, while his naked bride sleeps on. In the end, the man becomes a faithful hermit serving María until she takes him to Paradise. Ironically, it appears the young man never

---

[10] "42," in *Songs of Holy Mary*, 55. In *galego dedo con el*," *Cantigas de Santa María* Database.

[11] *Songs of Holy Mary*, 55.

[12] The Cistercian monastery founded by Bernard in France. Considering Bernard's theologizing on Mary, this is not surprising.

[13] *Songs of Holy Mary*, 56.

gets to play ball, and he is not one of the players portrayed in the second panel.

The Text in Context

Cantiga 42 is one of three hundred and fifty-three miracle stories about the Mother of God recorded in the *Cantigas de Santa María*. Created during the thirteenth century in the court of Alfonso X, dubbed El Sabio, the Wise or Learned (1252–84 CE), "*Don Affonso de Castela, de Toledo, de Leon rey, e ben des Conpostela ta o reyno d'Aragon . . . ,*"[14] the *Cantigas* are among the largest, yet most overlooked, compilations of Marian miracle stories drawn from sources across the medieval Christian world as well as locally from the Iberian peninsula. This body of work, considered by scholars to be "a cultural project of great importance for medieval literature, music, and art, and for the history of patronage,"[15] remains on the margins of study primarily because its language of composition is not *castellano* but medieval *galego-portuguesa*, the language popular among troubadours in Spain and an ancestor of la lengua gallega de mis abuelos.[16]

---

[14] *Cantigas de Santa María, de Don Alfonso El Sabio,* ed. Leopoldo Augusto de Cueto, Volúmen 1 (Madrid: La Real Academia Española, 1889), 26. It is interesting to note that in the opening lines of the *Cantigas* the region of Galicia is indicated not by name but by reference to its most renowned pilgrimage site Santiago de Compostela. Readers unfamiliar with Alfonso X may find the following overview in English helpful. My inclusion of this resource does not imply that I concur with all of the author's conclusions: Robert I. Burns, SJ, "*Stupor Mundi*: Alfonso X of Castile, the Learned," in *Emperor of Culture: Alfonso X the Learned of Castile and His Thirteenth-Century Renaissance*, ed. Robert I. Burns, SJ (Philadelphia: University of Pennsylvania Press, 1990), the Library of Iberian Resources Online, https://libro.uca.edu/alfonso10/emperor.htm.

[15] "Introduction to the Cantigas de Santa Maria," *Cantigas de Santa Maria* Database, http://csm.mml.ox.ac.uk.

[16] See Scarborough, Introduction to *Songs of Holy Mary*, xx; Israel J.

The *Cantigas* are structured in a series of nine miracle stories bounded by a cantiga de loor, a hymn of praise.[17] The use of *galego-portuguesa* for sacred songs was novel in that it was the language normally associated with popular entertainment, such as love songs and satiric verse. Manuel Pedro Ferreira suggests that Alfonso intended the Cantigas for diversified audiences, "sometimes the courtly circle, but mostly the larger audiences connected to palace and cathedral as well as other urban and even rural populations" but in practice this was not realized.[18] The presentation of las cantigas, in multiple media, is interactive and engages the senses. The miniatures appeal to the visual; the music and rhythmic verse involve both the oral and aural; and the performative dimension underscores the claim that its originality rests in its ability to be contemplated, read, and heard at the same time.[19]

Katz and John E. Keller, Introduction to *Studies on the Cantigas de Santa Maria: Art, Music, and Poetry/Proceedings of the International Symposium on the Cantigas de Santa Maria of Alfonso X, el Sabio (1221–1284) in Commemoration of its 700th Anniversary Year—1981*, ed. Israel J. Katz and John E. Keller (Madison, WI: Hispanic Seminary of Medieval Studies, 1987), 2.

[17] The songs from 401 and following do not follow this pattern. These cantigas include a prologue to five Marian feast days (410); five Marian feasts, María's birth (411), Immaculate Conception (413), Annunciation (415), Purification (417), Assumption (419); and five Christological cantigas (423–27). See *Songs of Holy Mary*, 482–14; John E. Keller and Annette Grant Cash, *Daily Life Depicted in the Cantigas de Santa Maria* (Lexingto, KY: University Press of Kentucky, 1998), 2.

[18] Manuel Pedro Ferreira, "The Medieval Fate of the *Cantigas de Santa Maria*: Iberian Politics Meets Song," *Journal of the American Musicological Society* (2016) 69 (2): 332-333, https://www.academia.edu/28336502/The_Medieval_Fate_of_the_Cantigas_de_Santa_Maria_Iberian_Politics_Meets_Song

[19] María Rosa Fernández Peña, "Miniaturas de la Navidad en las Cantigas a Santa María, de Alfonso X el Sabio," in *La Natividad: Arte, Religiosidad y Tradiciones Populares*, ed. Francisco Javier Campos and Fernández

The verses narrate a Marian miracle, and the miniatures, with their captions, constitute a form of sequential art, telling the story across panels, reminiscent of contemporary graphic novels or comics.[20] These are separate texts, in the sense that each is complete and can function on its own to communicate the tale. Artistic license, media, and genre also may explain variations in detail, emphasis, and, as I propose, nuances in theological meaning. Each song contains a refrain, repeated after each stanza, a further testament to a performative intent instead of a private devotion. For some scholars of the *Cantigas* the repetition of the refrains reinforced "for the listening audience the abstract message concretized by the performed miracle"; it embraced listeners "within ritualized time and subsequently [stirred] them to a better understanding of the refrain's message."[21] I am not convinced that the message conveyed in these songs and illustrations is necessarily abstract. The repetitiveness may also suggest a participatory dimension that encourages interactivity with those who hear the music, similar to the way that graphic art presupposes a "reader [who] reconstructs a storyworld . . . that goes beyond what has been inscribed in the sequential and configured layout of the panels."[22]

---

de Sevilla (San Lorenzo de El Escorial, Madrid: Real Centro Universitario Escorial-María Cristina, Servicio de Publicaciones, 2009), 438 ("la gran originalidad de las Cantigas reside en que se pueden contemplar, leer y escuchar a la vez, como si se tratase de una grandiosa cantata escénica").

[20] *Cantigas* scholar John Keller also makes this observation in John E. Keller and Richard P. Kinkade, *Iconography in Medieval Spanish Literature* (Lexington, KY: University Press of Kentucky, 1984), 13. See also Charles L. Nelson, "Art and Visualization in the *Cantigas de Santa Maria*: How the Artists Worked," in *Studies on the Cantigas de Santa Maria*, 111–34.

[21] Dianne M. Wright, "Verbal and Visual Contexts of Performance in the *Cantigas de Santa Maria*," *Grand Valley Review* 20 (1999): 80, https://scholarworks.gvsu.edu/gvr/vol20/iss1/18/.

[22] Chris González, "Turf, Tags, and Territory: Spatiality in Jaime Hernandez's Vida Loca: The Death of Speedy Ortiz," *ImageTexT: Interdis-*

¡Play Ball! Rereading Cantiga 42 Latinamente

Building on Fernando Segovia's hermeneutics of otherness and engagement,[23] I recognize the otherness of the text and images of the *Cantigas* and specifically in Cantiga 42, as well as the influences of my situatedness on my subsequent interpretations of this distant relative in la familia de béisbol. In the spaces between otherness and familiarity, my engagement with the images and verse of Cantiga 42 is not comprehensive but constructive. Segovia cautions interpreters to recognize the impact of their complex social locations and to avoid imposing one's worldview on an equally complex text and context. For example, in his commentary on the figures depicted in the six panels, including the five ballplayers in panel two, John Keller observes: "Skin tones are natural, and every person depicted in the illumination is blond, no doubt because the miracle is supposed to have taken place in Germany."[24] Consider how this contemporary assessment betrays racial and ethnic biases and imposes stereotypical understandings of people in Spain and Germany. What exactly is "natural" skin color, let alone in the polychromatic context of the Iberian Peninsula, which includes North African, Visigothic, and Celtic genetic inheritances in its hybrid mix? If, as scholars including Keller contend, the miniatures are a rich display of daily life in medieval Spain, why do these light-complexioned people reflect a different geographic

---

ciplinary Comics Studies 7, no. 1 (2013): 7, https://imagetextjournal.com/turf-tags-and-territory-spatiality-in-jaime-hernandezs-vida-loca-the-death-of-speedy-ortiz/

[23] Fernando F. Segovia, "The Text as Other: Toward a Hispanic American Hermeneutic," in *Text and Experience: Towards a Cultural Exegesis of the Bible,* ed. Daniel Smith-Christopher (Sheffield, UK: Sheffield Academic Press, 1995), 276–98.

[24] Keller and Kinkade, *Iconography in Medieval Spanish Literature*, 15.

context, unlike other similar figures in the *Cantigas* who portray the diversity of Spanish life?

Descriptions of the action in panel two that refer to baseball or employ terms such as outfielder, batter, and pitcher also reflect the situatedness of interpreters, because the text is ambiguous regarding the nature of the game. The verses mention playing ball (*"e jogavan à pelota," "por jogaren à pelot"*), and the hitting of the ball (*"feriss' a pelota"*). They provide no significant details of the game, and the artist of the miniature, by showing a player with a bat, interprets *un palo* as the means of hitting the ball in a manner that might do damage to a ring. The artist had other options available from the types of games that proliferated in la vida cotidiana. Scholars of Spanish sport explain that "ferir la pelota" refers to any number of these games, with a variety of ways of propelling the ball—by hand or foot or with an object external to the body.[25]

In the intertextual spaces it is possible for readers to imagine that Cantiga 42, through its narrative art, poetry, song, and storytelling, may well contribute to theologizing on sport, games, and play. I offer these provisional considerations as an initial foray into a rich and complex body of material that calls for further in-depth attention to lo popular beyond the immediate intention of this venture. These are first steps toward a retrieval of a multilayered source that reflects an option for culture and promises much vis-à-vis the interweaving of lived daily experience and its religious expressions and underpinnings.

The inclusion of play in las *Cantigas* is not a surprise. Scholars

---

[25] García García-Maroto and García González, "Patrimonio Histórico Español del Juego y del Deporte," ("'ferir la pelota' hace referencia a diversos ejercicios deportivos y competitivos muy presentes en la vida cotidiana de todos los grupos sociales, juegos consistentes en golpear, al aire o a ras de tierra, un objeto redondo con las manos, los pies o con ayuda de un palo u otro objeto").

suggest that the miniatures alone constitute one of the largest
detailed resources on medieval Iberian daily life, including count-
less images documenting recreational activity.[26] Even the miracle
tales are populated with accoutrements typical of thirteenth-
century Spain no matter the time frame or locale indicated in the
story. Theologically, these recognizable contemporaneous settings
reinforce the perception that ongoing accompaniment by the holy
occurs en lo cotidiano.

Alfonso demonstrated a predisposition to the ludic dimensions of daily life, evident in other undertakings, in particular, his
Libro de los juegos, a treatise on medieval board games, reflecting
the indisputable influence of Al-Andalus on Spanish life. The
Book of Games, like the *Cantigas*, was a long-term product from
his scriptorium with both text and illustrations. Alfonso begins
with an affirmation of the goodness of play, enumerating a variety
of physical activities that include "hitting the ball and other
games of many kinds in which men use their limbs in order to
make them strong and have fun."[27] He goes on to extol the virtues
of games that can be played from a seated position and indoors,
such as chess, tables, and dice. Such board games are accessible to
all sorts of people, including women who are confined or are not
equestrians, men with conditions such as age or weakness that
may limit their physical activity, those constricted by circumstances such as imprisonment, captivity, seafaring, or the vagaries
of weather.[28] For Alfonso games are a source of delight, a means

[26] For examples of recreational activity, see Keller and Grant Cash, *Daily Life*, 43–44.

[27] English translation of the prologue in portfolio 1 provided by Sonja Musser Golladay in "*Los Libros de Acedrex Dados e Tablas:* Historical, Artistic and Metaphysical Dimensions of Alfonso X's *Book of Games*" (PhD diss., University of Arizona, 2007), 106. *Libro de los Juegos* or the *Book of Games* commissioned by Alfonso X is known by several names including *Los Libros de Acedrex Dados e Tablas, The Books of Chess, Dice and Tables*.

[28] Musser Golladay, 106.

for people to amuse and comfort themselves while avoiding idleness. They may be pragmatic in terms of skill development, but ultimately they exist "because God wanted that man have every manner of happiness, in himself naturally, so that he could suffer the cares and troubles when they came to them, therefore men sought out many ways that they could have this happiness completely."[29] In her comprehensive study of el *Libro de los juegos*, Sonja Musser Golladay adds yet another dimension to Alfonso's understanding of play by proposing that the board games and their strategies "allow human beings to visualize the workings of the cosmos, utilize the wisdom gleaned from these games and in due course, apply the knowledge in a practical sense to solve life's greater problems."[30]

Follow the Ball

I propose that the sequential illustrations of Cantiga 42 in the first through third panels are open to interpretation and offer brief theological insight on play consistent with Alfonso's positions articulated elsewhere in his writings and in the practices of daily life. In panel one workers are busy renovating the church after placing the statue of María outside, as the caption indicates "*Como lavravan huna eigreia et poseron a omage de Sancta Maria no portal.*"[31] While scholars focus on the workers, less attention is given to describing the statue. Mary is seated with the child on her lap. In her right hand is a golden object that appears to be a ball or orb. It rests lightly on the tips of her first three fingers in a manner that seems almost playful, as if she intends to toss it or teach her child how to pitch.[32] The child with right hand

---

[29] Musser Golladay, 106.
[30] Musser Golladay, 1223.
[31] "CSM Number: 42," *Cantigas de Santa Maria* Database.
[32] The statue portrayed in the miniature bears a striking resemblance

extended looks toward the ball.

In panel two, the players are playing their game with two golden-colored balls visible. One ball is in the air as "fielders" prepare to catch it, and the other is on the fingertips of the "pitcher" as if it is about to leave his hand toward the waiting "batter." The panel may be portraying a sequence of events, or showing two different games with a ball, or providing a clue about the nature of the game—pitch, hit, field the ball. In panel three, the statue of Mary is shown with her finger clenched around a ring. Changes in Mary's facial expression are evident in her eyes and mouth, and the focus of both the mother and child shifts from the orb in panel one to the suitor in panel three. It is possible that the artist is having a bit of fun tweaking the reader, and in the gap between panels one and two a viewer can imagine that María might well be throwing out the first ceremonial pitch in an ancestral baseball pickup game in the local park.[33] In his 2015 biography of Alfonso X, medieval historian Simon Doubleday interprets Cantiga 42 as a comedy "infused with an irrepressible sense of humor, gently satirizing pious cliché that was surely enhanced in performance."[34] His analysis suggests that the cantigas are consistent with Alfonso's philosophy of humor, running counter to classical and ecclesial

---

to the Madonna of Essen with respect to the eyes, the ball in the hand, and the child's apparent interest in the ball. The Madonna, the oldest existing full sculpture of Mary (980 CE), was part of the treasury of the Abbey of Essen, a monastery of secular canonesses of women from among the noble class. For a photograph of the statue, see "Essen muenster goldene Madonna," https://commons.wikimedia.org/wiki/File:Essen_muenster_goldene_madonna-4.jpg

[33] Thanks to my colleague Richard McCarron, associate professor of liturgy at Catholic Theological Union, for his perceptive insights regarding the golden object in the statue's hand.

[34] Simon R. Doubleday, *The Wise King: A Christian Prince, Muslim Spain and the Birth of the Renaissance* (New York: Basic Books, 2015), Kindle edition, loc. 1798–99.

thinking that perceived laughter as "dangerous and disruptive, disturbing the rightful order of things."[35] Doubleday situates Alfonso within a greater wave of comic spirit that was sweeping thirteenth-century European culture, evident in the courts of other rulers as well as among Franciscans who sought to take literally the counsel of their founder to laugh in the face of tormentors.[36]

In light of Alfonso's positive assessment of games as sources of joy and comfort, attested to in the song with the affirmation of ball playing being the favored game of many youth, what might be significant about the possibility that a ball connects panels one and two? If indeed ball playing was the preferred game of the young, the Word-made-flesh would surely have been schooled into play by his mother. María reacts to her context. In panel one, the statue is moved outdoors in the vicinity of the park where the locals come to relax and play. Play is part of being human and therefore an inclination assumed as part of the incarnation, precisely "because God wanted that man have every manner of happiness."[37]

Panel two, in the subtlety of its details, raises interesting suppositions about play as a social equalizer. In the image, three youth wear dark stockings and two wear red hosiery, a privilege reserved to royalty and troubadours—if gifted by nobility. Scholars speculate about what this fashion statement implies about the professions or social status of these players. Was this a mixed game that included nobility, troubadours, the sons of a king, or perhaps resistant youth defying fashion bans articulated in sumptuary laws?[38] What might that say about social interactions in daily life?

Was the fashion hinting at Alfonso's own participation in such games because in both the *Cantigas* and el *Libro de los juegos* he

---

[35] Doubleday, loc. 1808–9.
[36] Doubleday, loc. 1811–26.
[37] Musser Golladay, 106.
[38] See, for example, Keller and Grant Cash, *Daily Life*, 17.

is depicted in scarlet hose?[39] Certain recreational activities were reserved to the nobility, others to knights, and still others prohibited to clergy. In *Las Siete Partidas*, Alfonso's legal code, prelates are restricted from playing and/or witnessing an extensive list of physical and sedentary games, including ball, "which tend to interfere with their composure."[40] However, while ball playing is not specifically named, the code allows for the king to take recourse in games and other recreational activities, including listening to music and reading, in order to "take comfort when oppressed with care and affliction."[41] The sons of kings should also be shown "how to ride and hunt and play all kinds of games."[42]

If panels one and two affirm the goodness of play, then panels three through six put *homo ludens* into perspective. In the context of the greater story, Cantiga 42 presents the tale of a frivolous young man who wears commitments lightly. He is in love, yet risks losing a valuable symbol of that relationship in order to play ball. He is either flippant or genuinely captivated by the beauty of the statue, enough to forget his beloved for a second time, "from this

---

[39] In *Daily Life*, Keller and Grant Cash mention that only one of the fielders is wearing scarlet hose (17), but there are actually two players attired in this fashion with one leg of each clearly visible. A fraction of the left leg of the player in the forefront is barely visible toward the border of the panel. Musser Golladay notes that scarlet stockings were a mark of the king in both the *Cantigas* and el *Libro de los Juegos* (755). She lists cantigas where Alfonso is depicted in scarlet hosiery, see footnote no. 152, 755. She too cites Keller and Grant Cash and references sumptuary laws that addressed this issue.

[40] Alfonso X, "Title V, Law LVII," in *Las Siete Partidas: The Medieval Church*, ed. Robert I. Burns, SJ, trans. Samuel Parsons Scott (Philadelphia: University of Pennsylvania Press, 2001), 76–77. These restrictions on the clergy are curious in light of Alfonso's positive assessment of play, and they require further investigation beyond the parameters of this chapter.

[41] Alfonso X, "Title V, Law XXI," 297.

[42] Alfonso X, in "Title VII, Law X," 306.

day forth that lady whom I loved means nothing to me."[43] His promise to María quickly fades, and he returns to his first love, whom he then abandons for a third time on their wedding night, behavior that would certainly warrant scrutiny from a feminist perspective regarding Mary's complicity in abetting emotional infidelity and spousal abandonment. Or perhaps the one being saved in the miracle is the woman married to a man who "often changed his fancies."[44] In terms of sport, in both verse and graphics, ball playing is not the problem; rather, it is the player, who plays capriciously with relationships.

In the *Cantigas*, Latin@ theologians find a situated "author," a hybrid (born of a Castilian father and a German mother, raised in Galicia by surrogates), living and leading in a pluricultural, multiethnic, polylingual, interreligious context. In image and text, Alfonso emerges as a king, patron, poet, devoted supplicant in need of aid, and self-defined troubadour of María, who asserts, "I wish from this day forth to be Her troubadour, and I pray that She will have me for Her troubadour and accept my songs, for through them I seek to reveal the miracles she performed."[45] His strengths and human frailties are represented in word and image, and Cantiga 42, with its repentant suitor, may well be a metaphor for the life of the king, who, through las *Cantigas*, chooses "to sing for no other lady, and I think thereby to recover all that I have wasted on the others."[46] Scholars such as Joseph Snow see in the *Cantigas* a spiritual autobiography recasting Alfonso in a personal quest for salvation, "as the model, the troubadour who would lead other troubadours, the sinner who would turn other sinners onto the upward path toward the greater reward" through Mary.[47] Connie

---

[43] *Songs of Holy Mary*, 55.

[44] *Songs of Holy Mary*, 55.

[45] "B," *Songs of Holy Mary*, 2.

[46] *Songs of Holy Mary*, 2.

[47] See, for example, Joseph T. Snow, "Alfonso as Troubadour: The

Scarborough pursues this trajectory with an intriguing twist. She proposes that Alfonso positions himself between heaven and earth as a priest-mediator and the *Cantigas* function as a penitential text with the miracle stories "illustrating examples of grace and forgiveness for a myriad of sins."[48]

I propose that Alfonso also envisions himself as teacher and a theologian who uses the milagros y loors to articulate a textured theology of María and that the art of Cantiga 42 alludes to his theologizing on games and play. In the *Cantigas'* miniatures Alfonso is often portrayed with a book and never with a sword, the symbol of a king's authority.[49] Such iconography situates him actively in the creative process in multiple roles. I contend that the presence of a book points not only to the product but implies a didactic function reminiscent of the portrayal of the evangelists in their roles as theologians and teachers through their gospels. If Cantiga 42 may also be understood as a metaphor for the king's life, then the hermit devoted to María in panel six, with open book facing outward, signals not only Alfonso's scholarliness, or his massive creative multimedia product, but teaches the lessons learned by the king as articulated in the refrain of the cantiga: "The most glorious Virgin, spiritual queen, is possessive (jealous) of those she loves, because she does not want them to do wrong [*A Virgen mui groriosa, Rea espirital, dos que ama é ceosa, ca non quer que façan mal*]."[50] Adherence in service to the Mother of God

Fact and the Fiction," in *Emperor of Culture*; Joseph T. Snow, "Alfonso X retratado en las *Cantigas de Santa Maria*," *Concentus Libri* 4 (April 1998): 82–86, http://www.concentus.es/c024.htm.

   [48] Connie L. Scarborough, "The *Cantigas de Santa María* as Penitential Text," in *Actas do segundo congreso de estudios Galegos: Homenaxe a José Amor y Vázquez*, ed. Antonio Carreño (Vigo, ES: Galaxia, 1991), 137.

   [49] Joseph F. O'Callaghan, *Alfonso X and the Cantigas de Santa Maria: A Poetic Biography* (Leiden: Brill, 1998), 70.

   [50] Kulp-Hill translates "*ceosa*" (celosa in Spanish) as "solicitous" instead of "jealous" or "zealous." Based on the actions of María (as statue and in

results in what the poet believes and knows to be true—that María will bring them with her "from this world to Paradise, the Heavenly realm."[51] Therefore, play, while good, and a source of joy and comfort, is best exercised in moderation so as not to distract one from the true and eternal source of comfort and joy.

Bridging Playgrounds:
From Medieval Spain to the United States

The *Cantigas* engage lo popular in content, style, media, and vernacular. They serve, individually and collectively, as an inexhaustible example of the fluidity and porousness of popular religion and popular culture, a challenge to the imposition of categories that artificially distinguish between sacred and profane. In these ways, across the centuries, las *Cantigas* connect with striking familiarity by recognizing lo cotidiano, daily living, as locus for all activity: divine, political, creative, mundane. They resonate with a stream of Latin@ theologizing that plays on and in the margins with the stuff of life, making preferential options for culture in all of its complexity and expressions. From this vantage point, the emperor of culture, who was also the king of Santiago de Compostela, merits greater in-depth study, a retrieval from the margins that cannot be naïve or romanticized, nor disconnected from discourses about power, privilege, and the complex tensions of medieval Iberian convivencia and the reconquista.

Cantiga 42 and panel two in particular have been

---

person) in both verse and art, I contend that "solicitous" is too mild. In the context of Cantiga 42, I would interpret *ceosa* as a possessive, jealous love manifest in a zealous desire to protect those she loves from doing wrong. Thanks to my colleague Latin@ biblical scholar and theologian Jean-Pierre Ruiz for his insights in translating *galego* into English and Spanish.

[51] *Songs of Holy Mary*, 56.

contemplated with some frequency by English-language dominant scholars, so much so that a sketch of that panel of ballplayers by Charles Nelson graces the cover of the first complete English translation of the *Cantigas* by Kathleen Kulp-Hill.[52] This illustration for the *Songs of Holy Mary* led to an inquiry that set in motion the acquisition of the reproduction of panel two by the historian of the National Baseball Hall of Fame in Cooperstown.[53] The image remains on the margins of baseball scholarship as well. I suspect this is partly because of its Spanish sourcing, its explicitly religious context, and, because in the United States, the focus has long been on either establishing or challenging the supposed English roots of the "American pastime," a consequence of a conflicted relationship between the United States and its former colonial master.[54]

---

[52] Cantiga 42 is highlighted in the work of a number of English-language scholars; see, for example, Keller and Kinkade, *Iconography in Medieval Spanish Literature*, 13–20; John E. Keller, "The Threefold Impact of the *Cantigas de Santa Maria*: Visual, Verbal, and Musical," in *Studies on the Cantigas de Santa Maria*, 26–30; Wright, "Verbal and Visual Contexts of Performance in the *Cantigas de Santa Maria*," 81–83.

[53] Connie L. Scarborough, "Recent Scholarship on the *Cantigas de Santa Maria*," *Alcanate* 2 (2000): 264, https://idus.us.es/handle/11441/82537. Scarborough records that Cooperstown wanted a copy of the panel for their archive. A reproduction of panel two was hanging in a gallery when I visited the National Baseball Hall of Fame and Museum in May 2013.

[54] See, for example, Albert Goodwill Spalding, *America's National Game: Historic Facts concerning the Beginning, Evolution, Development and Popularity of Base Ball, with Personal Reminiscences of Its Vicissitudes, Its Victories and Its Votaries* (New York: American Sports, 1911); Robert W. Henderson, *Ball, Bat and Bishop: The Origin of Ball Games* (1947) (Urbana, IL: University of Illinois Press, 2001); David Block, *Baseball before We Knew It: A Search for the Roots of the Game* (Lincoln, NE: University of Nebraska Press, 2005).

In the greater context of play, it cannot be forgotten that games designed for fun, like "hitting the ball," or board games that provided consolation, or sport based on skill with weapons did not only function to amuse, comfort, and provide a remedy for idleness.[55] Games and play also served a martial purpose, preparing men physically and mentally for war and conquest. In the late nineteenth and twentieth centuries, baseball became entwined in the fabrication of a mythology of American exceptionalism that binds up the sport with an imperial legacy of racism, conquest, colonization, and Christian mission especially in Latin America. As part of a larger "civilizing" project, baseball was used in efforts to refashion the colonized other into an Americanized Christian image yet without the power, privilege, access, or citizenship status such an image implied.[56] This evangelization, both at home and abroad, continues to communicate particular theologies of nation to this day.

---

[55] Musser Golladay, 107.

[56] Carmen M. Nanko-Fernández, "¿Dios bendiga whose América? Resisting the Ritual Theologizing of Nation," updated and reprinted in *Religion and Sport in North America: Critical Essays for the Twenty-First Century*, eds. Randall Balmer and Jeffrey Scholes (London, UK and New York, NY: Routledge, 2023), 246-275.

Index

Academy of Catholic Hispanic Theologians of the U.S. (ACHTUS), 28

acompañamiento, theology of, 61–63, 68

adaptatio-accomodatio concept, wide adoption of, xxiii

Alfonso X of Castile
Cantigas de Santa Maria, as author of, 99–100
Las Siete Partidas legal code, 108
Libro de los juegos, penning, 104–5, 107
philosophy of humor, 106–7
as a teacher and theologian, 110
as a troubadour of María, 109

Bailey, Randall, 30

baseball
American exceptionalism as entwined with mythology of, 113
ancestral baseball in medieval Spain, 97, 103, 106
as a metaphor of existence, 95–96

National Baseball Hall of Fame, 96, 112

Benedetti, Mario, 31

Brenner, Athalya, 36

Bronner, Leila Leah, 42

Building Bridges: Doing Justice: Constructing a Latino/a Ecumenical Theology, 28

Bush, George W., 51, 55

Caminemos con Jesús (Goizueta), 61, 63

Cantigas de Santa María
bat and ball game, miniatures portraying, 97–98, 103, 112
lo cotidano, recognizing, 104, 111
as medieval Marian miracle stories, 96, 99–102
play, theological insights on, 105–11, 112–13

cartographic approach to theology
culture wars as a factor, 57
Latino/a theologies and the cartographic task, 67–69
the margins, presence required at, 60, 63

CONTRIBUTORS

María Teresa (MT) Dávila is Associate Professor of Practice and Chair of the Department of Religious and Theological Studies at Merrimack College, North Andover MA. Her work focuses on the areas of migrant and racial justice, the option for the poor and Catholic social teaching, the ethics of the use of force, and public theology. With Agnes Brazal, she is co-editor of *Living With(out) Borders: Theological Ethics and Peoples on the Move* (Orbis, 2016). Her work appears regularly in the Theology en la Plaza column in the *National Catholic Reporter*, *Syndicate*, and *Political Theology Today*. She is a Roman Catholic laywoman.

Miguel H. Díaz is the John Courtney Murray, S.J., University Chair in Public Service at Loyola University Chicago. Dr. Díaz served under President Barack Obama as the 9th U.S. Ambassador to the Holy See. He is a co-editor of the series *Disruptive Cartographers: Doing Theology Latinamente*. He is editor of the multi-authored volume one, *The Word Became Culture* and the author of the third volume, *Queer God de Amor* (Fordham University Press, 2022). As a public theologian, Professor Díaz regularly engages print, radio, and television media. He is a contributor to the Theology en la Plaza column for the *National Catholic Reporter*. As part of his ongoing commitment to advance human rights globally, he participates in a number of diplomatic initiatives in Washington, D.C., including being a member of the Atlantic Council and a member of the Ambassadors Circle at the National Democratic Institute (NDI).

Néstor Medina is a Guatemalan-Canadian Scholar and associate professor of Religious Ethics and Culture at Emmanuel College of Victoria University in the University of Toronto. He engages the field of ethics from contextual, liberationist, intercultural, and post and decolonial perspectives. He studies the intersections between people's cultures, histories, ethnoracial relations, and forms of knowledge in religious and theoethical traditions. He also studies Pentecostalism in the Americas. Among his publications, Medina is the author of Christianity, Empire and the Spirit (Brill, 2018), On the Doctrine of Discovery (CCC, 2017), a booklet, and Mestizaje: (Re)Mapping 'Race,' Culture, and Faith in Latina/o Catholicism (Orbis, 2009), which was the winner of the 2012 Hispanic Theological Initiative book award.

Carmen M. Nanko-Fernández is Professor of Hispanic Theology and Ministry and the director of the Hispanic Theology and Ministry Program at the Catholic Theological Union in Chicago. A Latin@ theologian, her publications include the book *Theologizing en Espanglish* (Orbis, 2010), as well as numerous chapters, scholarly and pastoral articles on Latin@ theologies, theological education, *lo popular*, sport and theology—with particular focus on béisbol/baseball and Pope Francis on sports. She created, coordinates, and is an author for the Theology en la Plaza column in the *National Catholic Reporter* and her writing has appeared in *Commonweal*. The founding co-editor of the multivolume series *Disruptive Cartographers: Doing Theology Latinamente*, she is also completing her book *¿El Santo? Baseball and the Canonization of Roberto Clemente* (Mercer University Press). A past president of the Academy of Catholic Hispanic Theologians of the United States (ACHTUS), she received their Virgilio Elizondo Award for distinguished achievement in theology.

Cardinal Gianfranco Ravasi is President emeritus of the Pontifical Council for Culture and President of the Pontifical Commission for Sacred Archeology. A professor of exegesis of the Old Testament, he taught in Milan at Facoltà Teologica dell'Italia Settentrionale and from 1989 to 2007 he served as prefect of the Ambrosian Library. Since March 2012 he has been president of the cultural association Casa di Dante in Rome, dedicated to making the works of Dante known throughout Italy and abroad. In 2011, he inaugurated the initiative, "The Court of the Gentiles, which earned him international acclaim. This initiative sought to bridge Christian faith and reason by engaging in critical conversations with a wide range of publics. He is a prolific writer who has authored some 150 volumes, mostly in biblical studies, as well as numerous popular publications.

Jean-Pierre Ruiz teaches on the faculty of the Department of Theology and Religious Studies at St. John's University in New York, where he is also a senior research fellow of the Vincentian Center for Church and Society. A noted Nuyorican biblical scholar and theologian, his publications also include the Catholic Press Association Award-winning book, *Readings from the Edges: The Bible and People on the Move* (Orbis, 2011). A past-president of the Academy of Catholic Hispanic Theologians of the U.S. (ACHTUS), he received their Virgilio Elizondo Award for distinguished achievement in theology. During the Obama administration, Ruiz served as a member of the U.S. Department of State's Working Group on Religion and Foreign Policy. Ruiz's current research interests include the Apocalypse of John, the place of the Bible in the colonization of the Americas, the Bible and migration, and interreligious dialogue (especially Jewish-Christian dialogue).